KNOWING
THE
SATISFIED GOD

Rabon Byrd

Transcription/Editing: Rachael Gibson

ISBN: 978-1479320264

Copyright – 2012 *U.S. Library of Congress*

The International Fellowship of Covenant Ministries
P.O. Box 446
3740 Trace Ridge Road
Leslie, Arkansas 72645

www.cmintl.org
Visit the above website for weekly Live Streaming Bible Classes.

cmibrc@yahoo.com
Author's contact- rabonbyrd@gmail.com

Table of Contents

Chapter One
A Satisfied God ~ Our Beginning — 01

Chapter Two
The Basis of The Spirit's Work — 37

Chapter Three
...But When It Pleased God — 77

Chapter Four
Christ In You The Fulfillment of All things — 109

Chapter Five
Salvation: A Matter of Apprehension — 139

Chapter Six
Comparing Spiritual Things with Spiritual — 169

Chapter Seven
Cast Not Away Your Confidence — 187

Chapter Eight
The Answer of a Good Conscience — 213

All references are from the King James Version unless otherwise noted.

PREFACE

Satisfied is a comprehensive and weighty term. When you look this word up in the dictionary, it speaks of being fully pleased because something desired and anticipated has been accomplished as desired. When searching the etymology of the word satisfied, it is very interesting that it evolved from the Latin contentus, which means contained. The Online Etymology Dictionary elaborates by stating that the word evolved from "contained," or "restrained," to "satisfied," but continues to convey the thought that the contented person's desires are bound by what he or she already has. This means that the satisfaction of the person is contained and bound within the content he already possesses. That person needs nothing more added to what is already possessed in order to be satisfied. That is exactly what I mean by The Satisfied God. God has in His possession the totality of His eternal delight contained within the person of His Son and there is nothing that needs to be or can be added. The grace of God now permits the soul of man to know and partake of that One in whom the entirety of the eternal satisfaction of God is contained.

Unfortunately, that understanding seems to be altogether absent in the Christian world. Therefore, when using the term satisfied with relation to God the Father, it is essential that we establish the single object of His satisfaction, so that we do not live with a false expectation with regard to our relationship and standing with God. Religion sets forth the false concept that God looks at man and his religious deeds in order to find His satisfaction. Such a self-centered view of salvation and God's perspective keeps the soul in a continuous state of condemnation and dissatisfaction. T. Austin Sparks says it beautifully in his book, *The School of Christ*. He writes, *"We cannot produce from this nature anything acceptable to God. All that can ever come to God is in Christ alone, not in us. It never will, in this life, be in us as ours. It will always be the difference between Christ and ourselves. Though He be resident within us, He and He only is the object of the Divine good pleasure and satisfaction. And the one basic lesson you and I have to learn in this life, under the Holy Spirit's tuition, revelation, and discipline is that He is other than we are....When you have come to your best, there is still a gulf between you and the beginnings of Christ that cannot be bridged."* This is an excellent thesis statement for this book, so keep it in mind as you proceed.

I will ask a question in this book that is very important to consider, for the answer will determine everything with regard to your walk in Christ. Where do you look to find the evidence of a perfect salvation? Most of us will explicitly deny that we look at ourselves to find perfection. However, that seems to be the objective of most religious activities. We implement accepted observances in order to remedy the imperfections and maladies we observe in ourselves. This is because there is still some residual hope that one day we will finally reach a condition where God will be able to observe us and give an assuring nod of pleasure in our direction. In this book, it is my desire to present to you the Man and Face unto which God the Father looks to find divine perfection; the One to whom He can and has eternally said, *"This is my beloved Son, in whom I am well pleased."* The Spirit of God desires to bring us face to face with the sole object of God's eternal delight, so that we may experience satisfaction and rest for the soul as God has defined it from before the foundation of the world. The work of God is to reveal and establish His view, His understanding, and His satisfaction in the soul of all who are born of the Spirit of Christ, so that we may also be satisfied with what we already possess. It is my prayer that this book will be a tool used of the Father, to do that work within the heart of every reader.

Rabon Byrd
September 2012

CHAPTER ONE

A SATISFIED GOD – OUR BEGINNING

Born Again! It is such a glorious gift of the Grace of God to be able to utter those words. How wonderful it is to know that we have been given and have dwelling in our hearts a full salvation and, as a result, we are in right standing with God. Unfortunately, to the majority of Christians, that view of salvation is absent. To most, we have sins forgiven and the promise of a glorious future. The Christian's typical understanding of right standing with God seems to change from day to day, depending upon how well they feel they have performed the prescribed Christian duties. The thought that I am attempting to convey to you is that most who are born again have no idea what that means. Therefore, they are not experiencing that full, complete, and perfect salvation of which I am speaking. I trust that you will not misunderstand me but it is not enough to be born again. Let me make it clear that if you are born again you have been given all things[1] and have been blessed with all spiritual blessing in heaven, in Christ, and about that there

---

[1] 2 Peter 1:3
Seeing that His divine power has granted to us everything pertaining to life and godliness, through the true knowledge of Him who called us by His own glory and excellence. - NASB

is no doubt or dispute.[2] However, that is not sufficient as to our growing up in the knowledge and apprehension of that grand reality. Paul writes in 2 Timothy 2:10, *"Therefore I endure all things for the elect's sakes, that they may also obtain the salvation which is in Christ Jesus with eternal glory."* When we read the term "obtain," we may think that Paul is speaking of the believer receiving something not yet given. Yet in the Greek, that is not the meaning of this term and is not the intent of the statement. Remember, Paul is writing here concerning his heart toward those in Christ. So they *already have* received this salvation in Christ with eternal glory. The meaning of this term "obtain" in the Greek is *"to experience and enjoy something that is already happening."*[3] Accordingly, the proper translation of this verse is ἵνα καὶ αὐτοὶ σωτηρίας τύχωσιν τῆς ἐν Χριστῷ Ἰησοῦ - *"in order that even these might experience the salvation which is in Jesus Christ."* Paul understands that what is vital for the Body of Christ is not receiving something that is lacking, because there is nothing lacking with regard to our salvation. His reason for preaching the gospel and facing the gruesome things he faced was that the Body of Christ, having been given the salvation that is in Christ that has bound up within itself eternal glory, would come to an inward experiencing of that which they have already been given of God in Christ. He desired the Church to know the full measure of their Great Salvation. Regardless of what is taught today, there is nothing lacking with regard to your salvation, but there is an experiencing and enjoyment of salvation lacking in the hearts of most

---

[2] Ephesians 1:3
Blessed [is] the God and Father of our Lord Jesus Christ, who did bless us in every spiritual blessing in the heavenly places in Christ. – YLT

[3] Greek-English Lexicon Based on Semantic Domain. Copyright © 1988 United Bible Societies, New York. Used by permission

Christians. The experiencing of that salvation only comes in the revealed presence of the indwelling Christ and that brings about innumerable effects in the soul. However, at this point we need at least to settle in our hearts that the salvation given of God is perfect and the Spirit of God desires to work in us toward the experiencing and enjoyment of it. We will touch later upon the fact that the Spirit of God alone can bring about such a satisfaction into the soul. I must share with you that the word "obtain" again carries with it the meaning *to hit upon and obtain unto our satisfaction.* [4] It is my desire in writing this book for the Church to come to experience salvation in a manner that brings about the satisfaction of the soul. In reality, the one cannot be happening without the other, but that will be understood as we proceed.

You will see in this small offering that I will not present you with steps to reach that state of satisfaction. I cannot do that. At one point, I realized that even Paul could not do that. Paul, the man in whom God introduced the New Covenant by revealing the Son,[5] could only declare the reality that he was beholding in Christ. In Ephesians, he beautifully writes to them concerning the fact that God has summed up, comprehended, and gathered all things in heaven and earth in His Son. Upon the heels of that wonderful declaration of reality, he does not proceed to give them the twelve steps that will cause them to know that eternal reality in a soul transforming way. Paul

---

[4] 5177 τυγχάνω Vine's Expository Dictionary of Biblical Words, Copyright © 1985, Thomas Nelson Publishers.

[5] Galatians 1:15-16
But when it pleased God, who separated me from my mother's womb, and called me by his grace, To reveal his Son in me, that I might preach him among the heathen; immediately I conferred not with flesh and blood.

proclaimed the reality as it is in Christ; the reality into which they had been brought as those who were accepted in the Beloved, but the declaration of that is as far as he could go. Paul related to them the objective reality, but he could not cause it to be a subjective work and acknowledgment within the soul. Therefore, his prayer for them was, *"That the God of our Lord Jesus Christ, the Father of glory, may give unto you the Spirit of wisdom and revelation in the knowledge of him: The eyes of your understanding being enlightened; that ye may know what is the hope of his calling, and what the riches of the glory of his inheritance in the saints."*[6] Notice how Paul begins this statement. That "God...may give unto you." The gospel always directs the soul toward that end. It will never be a call for the reader or hearer to remember what was said and to rehearse it in their mind until they understand the mystery that is being declared.

The mystery that is heralded by the preaching of the gospel cannot be acknowledged in that way. You can agree with true things and give mental and theological assent to them, but you will not inwardly grasp the spiritual reality they declare by that or any other external means. Paul's prayer was for them to submit their hearts and allow the Father of Glory to give unto them what only He can, because what He is giving is the light, knowledge, and understanding that is exclusively His own. He will reveal in your soul that Son in Whom He has gathered all things, for if you are born again, that is the One Who lives in you. Paul could and did declare the good news of a full and consummated salvation in Christ, but regardless of how excellent and profound his declaration, he could never cause them to inwardly apprehend and experience the Essential Being of the gospel and thus of salvation. He knew his limitations as a

---

[6] Ephesians 1:17-18

messenger of this glorious gospel, so having conveyed all that he had, he had to pray for them. Paul trusted that they would submit their souls to the Spirit of God so that He may give unto them the Spirit of revelation in the knowledge of Christ, that the eyes of their souls would be filled and flooded with the light of the knowledge of the glory of God in the face of Jesus Christ.

That is all that we who preach the gospel can do. Those speaking and those hearing the gospel are mutually dependent on the work of the Spirit called the Revelation of Jesus Christ. I do not mean God revealing to us better theological ideas through the scripture. For many years after being born again, I heard revelation being defined as God giving a better thought with regard to a certain portion of scripture. However, what was called "revelation" was just the puffed up thoughts of man, because it seemed to always bring man into a greater focus and make him the center of all things. They would add their ego and intellect to the scriptures and end up with another gospel, which is not another. The Revelation of Christ in the soul leaves no room for our doctrinal statements and our theological ideas. The Revelation of Jesus Christ leaves no room for anything but Christ! The grace of God, which has made Christ to be unto us all things, leaves no room for anything or anyone, for it makes no provision for the flesh.[7] The gospel will never focus the heart upon self, for it can only declare the One God Himself accepts and receives. The gospel directs the heart to behold that One as our all. We must preach the gospel of grace to the Body of Christ.

---

[7] 1 Corinthians 1:30-31
But of him are ye in Christ Jesus, who of God is made unto us wisdom, and righteousness, and sanctification, and redemption: That, according as it is written, He that glorieth, let him glory in the Lord.

I realize how dangerous it is to use the phrase "The Gospel of Grace" unless those to whom you say it have the proper man in view. It seems that when this phrase or doctrinal thought is presented, it is predicated upon the false premise that grace is for the spiritual ascendance of man. What has happened? The wrong man is in view. Grace is not about man becoming like God or awakening to the notion that he is a "god." Grace, as well as all scriptural terms, must be seen in the context of the Cross, because in its truest definition grace is *"I am crucified with Christ: nevertheless I live; yet not I, but Christ liveth in me."* [8] Grace is not Christ empowering me to live for God or to live like God, but grace is 'not I, but Christ liveth in me.' That is the reason Paul, can say as one that has been experientially crucified with Christ, *"I do not frustrate the grace of God."* Because the frustration of the grace of God is our attempting to live unto God by the life that He has not given and therefore does not accept. It is also defined by the fact that, unlike in Paul's former manner of living, although he lives in a body of flesh, he no longer attempts to see the signs and evidences of righteousness or any other spiritual aspect in that body of flesh. Such an egocentric view of relationship with God frustrates God's grace. It frustrates God's grace because God's grace has brought us into union with Christ and has made Him to be in us the ALL of the all things that are of God in this New Creation.

With that being established, we will now proceed looking at God's satisfaction. The preceding statements are crucial for us to be aware of if we are going to truly know and experience the satisfaction of God. If we are attempting to comprehend the satisfaction of God while ignorant of the grace of which I have just written, we will always in our own hearts remain dissatisfied, because we will be

---

[8] Galatians 2:20

expecting God's satisfaction and pleasure to be found in and exhibited by ourselves. Again, the wrong man is in view. Grace has brought us into a living relationship with a satisfied God, but where is God's pleasure realized? I will no doubt repeat this. Although our God is eternally satisfied, it is possible and for most probable that we can live, even in Him, unsatisfied. I trust that as we progress in this book, God will use what is written to create a hunger in our hearts to know this satisfied God in the Light of the One who is His eternal delight. Dear reader, it is God's desire to give us His Light, so that we may see and experience His own satisfaction inwardly and apprehend Him as our own.

We will begin this search looking at various verses. At first, you may not understand the connection between these verses, but it will become obvious as we go.

Genesis 1:31, *"And God saw every thing that he had made, and, behold, it was very good. And the evening and the morning were the sixth day."* Genesis 2:1-3, *"Thus the heavens and the earth were finished, and all the host of them. And on the seventh day God ended his work which he had made; and he rested on the seventh day from all his work which he had made. And God blessed the seventh day, and sanctified it: because that in it he had rested from all his work which God created and made."* The grand significance of the Old Testament is that it declares in natural terms and by natural means a spiritual reality that was coming and now has come in Christ. It declares something spiritual and these verses are no different. God saw all that He had made (speaking of a finished work) and in view of that He said, "It is good in its entirety; it is very good." He then, having fulfilled His own desire and satisfying Himself, rested on the seventh day. Who is it that comes and declares, I AM the seventh day? I AM the

Sabbath! I AM the Rest of God! Jesus says in Matthew 11:27, *"All things are delivered unto me of my Father: and no man knoweth the Son, but the Father; neither knoweth any man the Father, save the Son, and he to whomsoever the Son will reveal him."* Now there is an exclusive relationship presented here between the Father and the Son, and the Cross has not made it any less exclusive. We think it has. I will point this out in a diagram, but it remains exclusive to the Father and the Son, and it never becomes anything less than that.

As I consider that, I realize how lost and how hopeless man is if not for the grace of God. There is no way in except God provide The Door.[9] There is no way in for us except He provide the Way.[10] Grace has abounded unto us in that we are in Christ, but grace has to be seen in the context of the proper man. It cannot be applied to Adam as if it is Adam receiving a spiritual life or even Adam being given a new lease on life, or a second chance before God. No, grace is that Adam no longer lives, but Christ lives in the soul. In other words, it is the fact that we do not have a relationship with God of our own. We have a relationship with God, but it is the one relationship in which God participates. God has brought us into that One Son with Whom He has always had relationship and now that Son is our relationship with the Father. It is not individual believers possessing relationships with God, but our souls being brought into and participating in the one relationship that is in the Beloved Son.

---

[9] John 10:9 I am the door: by me if any man enter in, he shall be saved, and shall go in and out, and find pasture.

[10] John 14:6 Jesus saith unto him, I am the way, the truth, and the life: no man cometh unto the Father, but by me.

It always puzzled me why such a declaration of love and relationship was made and then Jesus makes a seemingly unrelated statement in Matthew 11:28, *"Come unto me, all ye that labour and are heavy laden, and I will give you rest."* One day it finally dawned on me that if the relationship that is presented were not first an established reality, there would be no rest unto which He could call us. Primarily, Jesus is speaking here to those under the Law of Moses. In the confines of that system, they were attempting, by external means, to acquire an acceptable relationship with God. Jesus comes on the scene and presents Himself as the only one that has relationship with God and the only one with whom the Father has relationship. He is saying, "If you will come unto me and lay down your vain expectations of an independent relationship with God, I will bring you into "my own" relationship with my Father. The result of that will be nothing less than "rest for your souls." Your soul was created for that rest and only Christ can give it to you because He is the rest the Father Himself has found. This brings us back to God seeing all that He did and declaring it to be very good and in being satisfied, He rested on the seventh day. Here is Jesus saying, "If you will come unto Me, I will bring you to this rest, because I AM the finished work in which He is satisfied and I AM the place of His rest."[11] All things are done. It is perfect in the Father's House. The relationship, of which we are made partakers in Christ, needs NO additions. No additional work is necessary. The only work necessary is for the Spirit of God to enlighten the eyes of our souls and unveil our souls to the reality of that relationship Christ **is** within us. That may sound weird, but it will be clarified as we look at God's

---

[11] Psalms 132:13-14
For the Lord hath chosen Zion; he hath desired it for his habitation. This is my rest for ever: here will I dwell; for I have desired it.

eternal perspective being the view out from which He did and said all things.

In the light of that, we go to Matthew 3:14-17, *"But John forbad him, saying, I have need to be baptized of thee, and comest thou to me? And Jesus answering said unto him, Suffer it to be so now: for thus it becometh us to fulfil all righteousness. Then he suffered him. And Jesus, when he was baptized, went up straightway out of the water: and, lo, the heavens were opened unto him, and he saw the Spirit of God descending like a dove, and lighting upon him: And lo a voice from heaven, saying, This is my beloved Son, in whom I am well pleased."* Here God is pinpointing His will and delight in One Son. J.P. Greene's Literal Version brings in what I believe to be the most essential element in this declaration. The Literal Version reads, *"And behold! A voice out of the heaven saying, This is My Son, the Beloved, in whom I **have been delighting**."* That statement brings eternity into view. God is saying, "Here before you is the One in Whom I have eternally had my pleasure and delight. This is the One in whom my satisfaction has eternally been embodied." The phrase "In whom," sets a limit around and gives the full dimensions of the sphere of God's own satisfaction. This moment gives us the identity of the Wisdom of God, who speaks in Proverbs 8:30, declaring, *"I was daily his delight, rejoicing always before him [in his sight]."* Before that statement, it is significant that it is said in Proverbs 8:22-29, *"The Lord possessed me in the beginning of his way, before his works of old. I was set up from everlasting, from the beginning, or ever the earth was. When there were no depths, I was brought forth; when there were no fountains abounding with water. Before the mountains were settled, before the hills was I brought forth: While as yet he had not made the earth, nor the fields, nor the highest part of the dust of the world. When he prepared the heavens, I was there: when he set a compass upon the* *face of the depth: When he established the clouds above: when he strengthened the fountains of the deep: When he gave to the sea his decree, that the waters should not pass his commandment: when he appointed the foundations of the earth."* We will cover this again in a later chapter, but this speaks of the eternal Son as the delight and viewpoint of the Father, before anything that was made was made and in view of whom all that was made was made. So in Matthew 3:17, Jesus is declared as that very One unto whom the Father looked eternally and in whom His satisfaction has been forever personified. God never worked to accomplish something more than what He already had; He did all things out from the One that was always before Him. The grace of God is that He has made that One, who is the embodiment of His satisfaction, to dwell and live in us. What a salvation we have.

This should cause us to see the eternal significance of this declaration of the Father. According to J.P. Green, the exact same declaration (have been delighting) is spoken by the Father on the Mount when Jesus was transfigured.[12] If you will remember, it is in the light of this declaration from heaven that Peter declares, *"we have the more established prophetic Word."*[13] Peter is saying that the One that God revealed in the mountain, is the consummation of every word ever uttered and every type and figure ever given by God, because this is the One in view of whom every testimonial element and prophetic utterance was given. The satisfaction that God had before Him eternally is the One He revealed on that mountain. Moreover, that very same

---

[12] Matthew 17:5
While he was yet speaking, behold, a radiant cloud overshadowed them. And, behold, a voice out of the cloud saying, This is My Son, the Beloved, in whom I have been delighting; hear Him. – J.P. Green LITV

[13] J.P. Green LITV

Christ is the One that resides in our souls and we would do well to take heed unto Him that He might arise in our hearts as the Light of the Day of the Lord. All that is to say that the same One that God revealed on the mountain is the same One that God desires to reveal in us, so that we may know and enjoy His own eternal satisfaction.

Why is it that we insist on having a relationship with God or have God relate to us separately from the one relationship He has given in His Son? That same mindset would have us devising means to "be" the satisfaction of God's heart instead of beholding inwardly the One who is. We see one relationship exhibited in both the Law and Grace. In the following diagram, you will see a simple illustration of what I mean.

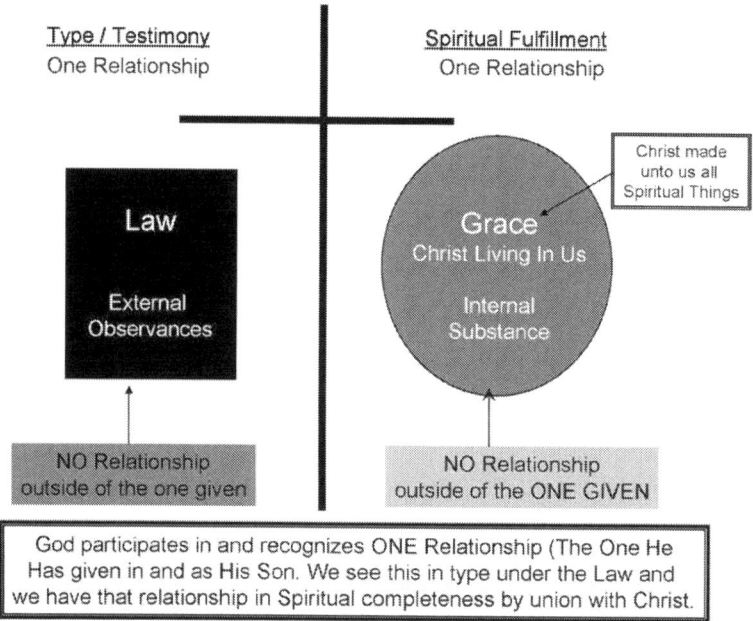

On one side of the Cross, you have the Law. The Law was a relationship given of God. To preface this we have to first state that God desired to be able to relate to Israel by faith, but they refused to do so. Therefore, He gave the Law to keep them by outward Law and ordinance, within the confines of a relationship that would only come to be perfected in Christ by faith. With that in mind, the illustration depicts how God related to man under the Law and He related to them in no other way. If they stepped outside of the boundaries of the Law, they were either killed or cast out of the camp - no relationship. This shows us that the only relationship that God accepted was the one He had given. I write these things trusting that you understand that the Law was a testimony of the Son and no ordinance and Law given was a means for man to possess their own relationship with God. The Law was God bringing them within the context of a physical and external system that spoke of the righteous Son with whom He eternally related. The only reason God was satisfied (figuratively but not literally) with that temporal relationship, was that it testified of the eternal relationship He had with His Son. However, in the New Covenant, God has not given us more external observations, which constrain us to external Laws. Grace is the very Life of Christ living in us as the spiritual intention and meaning of the Law, even the righteousness that satisfies the heart of the Father. However, it is still just one relationship. If you will recall, each individual Israelite did not have a little Ark of the Covenant in their tent. There was only ONE. They did not have a brazen altar in their individual tents. They had to bring their offering and sacrifice to the One altar, because God had set within them ONE relationship with Himself. That is what has taken place in us in spiritual fulfillment. God has placed in us the One relationship, the One Son that cries out within us, "Abba, Father". That is the One of whom He says, *"This is My Son, the Beloved, in whom I **have been delighting**."* If we are born of the Spirit, it is not given to us to become the object of God's pleasure, but we have been given the Son of God's eternal delight. It is that Son He desires to make known in us. This is so that Christ would not be in us crying, "Abba Father" and yet our souls fail to participate in that eternal communion.

Ephesians 1:3-5, *"Blessed be the God and Father of our Lord Jesus Christ, who hath blessed us with all spiritual blessings in heavenly places in Christ: According as he hath chosen us in him before the foundation of the world, that we should be holy and without blame before him in love: Having predestinated us unto the adoption of children by Jesus Christ to himself, according to the good pleasure of his will."*

First, let me briefly mention something concerning "predestination." Predestination has been wrongly defined because it has predominately been defined with the natural man in view. We must understand that predestination does not have man as its primary point of reference. How is that? Again, it goes back to God's eternal pleasure and perspective. The word predestination, in the Greek, actually means to "set boundaries before or in advance."[14] In other words, before God created anything, He defined and determined the boundaries, in which He would know, accept, and have relationship. He will not relate in any way to anyone or thing outside of these predetermined perimeters. Therefore, when we are born again we are brought into those predetermined boundaries wherein His delight and satisfaction is fully found. Paul uses the phrases, "IN Him, IN Christ, and IN the Beloved" many times in his letters. In doing that, he is not just using those terms as a catch phrase and he is not using them metaphorically. Paul used them because in his heart those

---

[14] NT:4309 προορίζω proorizo *(Biblesoft's New Exhaustive Strong's Numbers and Concordance with Expanded Greek-Hebrew Dictionary. Copyright © 1994, 2003, 2006 Biblesoft, Inc. and International Bible Translators, Inc.)*

phrases define the predestined realm of God's satisfaction and fulfillment in which the believer now resides. By using those phrases, Paul is presenting the fact that we will never find or experience anything of God's purpose, God's love, or God's salvation anywhere except within the confines of these defined borders. Paul tells the Galatians that he is amazed that they were removing themselves from Him that had called into the grace of Christ.[15] Literally, Paul is warning them that they are in the process of removing themselves from within the confines in which God relates to them, and that they are vainly attempting to relate to God in a way He does not accept. Most believers today are attempting, by religious zeal and exercise, to have a relationship with God that He does not recognize. That is precisely what religion presents as the goal unto which we are to reach. It is nothing more than the vain exercises of man offering God a counterfeit object. In reality, it is nothing more than neglecting the gift of His own satisfaction that He has already given and desires to make known in us.

Now we go to Colossians 1:12-19, *"Giving thanks unto the Father, which hath made us meet to be partakers of the inheritance of the saints in light: Who hath delivered us from the power of darkness, and hath translated us into the kingdom of his dear Son: In whom we have redemption through his blood, even the forgiveness of sins: Who is the image of the invisible God, the firstborn of every creature: For by him were all things created, that are in heaven, and that are in earth, visible and invisible, whether they be thrones, or dominions, or principalities, or powers: all things were created by him, and for him: And he is before all things, and by him all things consist. And he is the head of the body, the church: who is the beginning, the firstborn*

---

[15] Galatians 1:6

from the dead; that in all things he might have the preeminence. For it pleased the Father that in him should all fulness dwell." Also, Colossians 2:8-10, "Beware *lest any man spoil you through philosophy and vain deceit, after the tradition of men, after the rudiments of the world, and not after Christ. For in him dwelleth all the fulness of the Godhead bodily. And ye are complete in him, which is the head of all principality and power."*

Hebrews 1:1-4 from the New American Standard Version, *"God, after He spoke long ago to the fathers in the prophets, in many portions and in many ways, in these last days, hath spoken to us in Son, whom He appointed heir of all things, through whom He also made the world. And He (Christ) is the radiance of His glory, the exact representation of His nature, and upholds all things by the Word of His Power; when He had made purification of sin He sat down at the right hand of the Majesty on high; having become as much better than the angels as He has inherited a more excellent name than they."*

You may be wondering why I have shared these verses and you may not understand what they have in common. I have seen in these verses an underlying theme. In the beginning of this chapter, I stated that the motivating desire for writing this book is so that the Church, the Body of Christ, would come to experience and apprehend in their souls all that we have come to in Christ. So what have we come to? What is it that we have come to through our union with Christ? The reality is much different from what we have heard. I pose this question. What is our salvation? It is impossible to understand the greatness of our salvation until it becomes measured and defined in the Light of the greatness of the indwelling Christ. Understand, I am not referring to Christ afar off from us in the sky, but Christ in you. In view of the fact that Salvation is Christ in us, it stands that the fullness of our salvation can never be comprehended until it is defined and measured in the fullness of the indwelling Christ. The perfection of our salvation can never be defined except in the Light of the perfection of the indwelling Christ. HE IS ALL! Salvation must be, in our hearts, defined in Him, and measured in the Light of Him. That is nothing new to God because that is how He has always defined our salvation. That may be a shock to us, but in God's view it has always been Christ and it has always been IN HIM in intention, in testimony, and in fulfillment. We complicate the matter by attempting to bring ourselves into it and immediately our hearts are deviated from *the simplicity or singleness of Christ.*[16]

The majority of Christians have no idea what they have come to by new birth. Salvation has never been properly measured or defined in their hearts; and although we desire it, God does not define or measure salvation by looking at man.

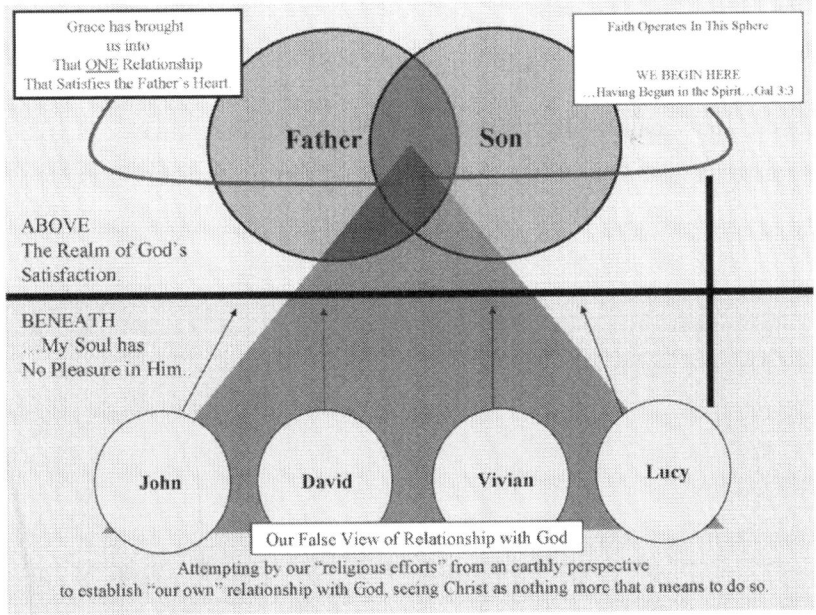

---

[16] 2 Corinthians 11:3

I have illustrated this in the diagram above. We have the two realms of which the scripture speaks. We have the terms above and beneath. In the scripture, the same distinction is made by the contrasting terms earth and heaven. In the "beneath" realm there are individual believers attempting to gain spiritual enhancement and establish "their own" standing with God by what they feel are acceptable means. Notice, there is a great dividing line here called the Cross. I want to stress that what is seen "beneath" is a false view of salvation. The view of salvation possessed by most is that we are individually attempting to please God by efforts and observances. We being ignorant of grace, attempt to use Christ as a means to present ourselves as acceptable to God. The triangle shows us that grace has brought us into the only acceptable and recognized relationship that is above. This is the eternal relationship of the Father and His Beloved Son and the only relationship in which God involves Himself. This is the proper view of salvation, for it is not I that pleases or satisfies God, but my soul being caught up into a living union with the Son who is His pleasure.

Religion promises the tools and the ability; it presents steps. However, the reality of our salvation is that God has already blessed us with all spiritual blessing in heaven in Christ; that means God has given us access into a relationship with Himself we could never have except for His grace! That is the beginning point. Salvation is not our beginning beneath and working our way above. We do not begin in a state of separation and work our way into union or into relationship with God. We begin in relationship with God, but **not our own**. We begin in the One relationship in which God eternally involves Himself.

Having written all of this, I ask again, "What have we come to in Christ?" What is salvation? I begin answering that by presenting to you what I believe all of our previous verses have in common. It is very simple. Every one of them declares a satisfied God. If you will notice, that satisfaction, in every case, did not have man as its object. You do not hear that much today because religion erroneously concludes that God has to be satisfied with man, so we had better do what we have to do to make God satisfied. In contrast to religion, the gospel declares God has been and is satisfied in His Son, and grace has made us partakers of His own satisfaction by union with that Son. That is what we have come to in Christ. That is salvation. There is no need on our part to attempt to add to or supplement that Son. He looked at what He had done in His creation and said 'It is very good.' If that is so with the natural creation that gives testimony, how much greater is that statement fulfilled in the Son who is Head and substance of the New Creation. Matthew 17:15 says the same thing. *"This is My Beloved Son, in whom I have been eternally delighting."* He could just as easily have said He is very good! He is the end of my work, He is the Sabbath in which I find my rest, He is my eternal satisfaction, – and it is very good!

On the mountain, Peter was attempting to hold onto the law, prophets, and Jesus, proposing to build three tabernacles, one for each of them. God did not allow such to occur. God's view is single – very specific – it is Christ! God is saying, "This is the One in whom I have been delighting eternally. He is the delight of my soul who Moses and Elijah, the Law and the prophets declared would come. He has come. Hear ye HIM! I have nothing else to say. I have no more works to perform." That is true, for even the miraculous works God performed through the ages and even through Jesus, pointed them to the reality that would be brought about in the Cross. That is why Jesus tells them when coming down the mountain to tell no one the vision until after the resurrection.[17] Then we read Paul declaring that it pleased God that in Him, all fullness should dwell, but he did not leave us out! In connection to that, in Him, you are complete; in Him, you are brought into the full and perfect satisfaction of the Father. That is where we begin. We begin with a satisfied God.

This is impossible for the natural mind to understand or accept. We begin with a satisfied God. We do not have to work and labor by whatever means we deem necessary to satisfy Him. He is satisfied! The grace of God is not Him giving you the ability to satisfy Him. The grace of God is the fact that He has brought you into His own satisfaction. He says to you, "If you will only just turn to see, I will share with your soul the satisfaction that already dwells in it." That is what God does. That is why faith works above and not beneath. We think faith gives individuals the ability to reach a right standing with God. However, faith is not a means to reach an acceptable standing with God. Faith beholds the reality that is already established above. Romans 5:2, *"By whom also we have access by faith into this grace wherein we stand."* We have access by faith into the grace wherein we presently stand. He is saying you are already standing in grace. That is the same as saying you are already standing in Christ. However, it is faith that establishes your heart there. The word "access" in this verse is very important. In the Greek, the word access is made up of two words: ago ἄγω, which means to bring or to be brought, and pros πρός which means to a facing, to the face or presence of. The word "access" then means to bring to the face or into the presence. It is by faith that we are

---

[17] Matthew 17:9 And as they came down from the mountain, Jesus charged them, saying, Tell the vision to no man, until the Son of man be risen again from the dead.

brought to the face of Him who is the grace in which we stand. That is why in Christ, it is by faith we walk, not by sight.[18] Faith does not get us to a state of being that we do not presently have. Faith comes into the soul and causes the soul to behold the Lord, and thus establishes that soul within those eternally defined borders of God's grace. Grace has brought us in and faith establishes our hearts where we are and keeps our hearts steadfastly beholding that Son in whom God is fully satisfied. What a glorious work of God. What a liberty it is to see that the satisfaction of God is not I, but Christ who lives within. That is why I titled this book, *Knowing the Satisfied God*. Salvation is God permitting the soul to partake of and participate in His own satisfaction. That is our salvation.

If you read Hebrews 10 in the context of *"Lo, I come, in the volume of the book it is written of Me,"*[19] you will see that Christ is declaring Himself to be the eternal satisfaction in view of whom and concerning whom every word of scripture has been written. It goes on to read, *"In sacrifices and offerings you had no pleasure."* They testified of the One who satisfied Him, but in those things themselves (external elements of the testimony), God was never satisfied, for His satisfaction was the Son in view of whom they were all given. So He says, *"Lo, I come to do your will."* The word "do" according to one Greek study means

---

[18] 2 Corinthians 5:7   For we walk by faith, not by sight.

[19] Hebrews 10:5-9
Wherefore when he cometh into the world, he saith, Sacrifice and offering thou wouldest not, but a body hast thou prepared me: In burnt offerings and sacrifices for sin thou hast had no pleasure. Then said I, Lo, I come (in the volume of the book it is written of me,) to do thy will, O God. Above when he said, Sacrifice and offering and burnt offerings and offering for sin thou wouldest not, neither hadst pleasure therein; which are offered by the Law; Then said he, Lo, I come to do thy will, O God. He taketh away the first, that he may establish the second.

to do whatever it takes to bring satisfaction to the heart. "I am come to satisfy your will." So what did it take to bring satisfaction to God's eternal will? "Lo I come." Let me address this for a moment. His coming did not make Him God's satisfaction or the object of God's pleasure or the satisfaction of God's own will, He came **as** the satisfaction of God. He appeared as who He eternally is. God's satisfaction was made known in His coming. In His coming, one entire age, humanity, and creation was removed and the risen Son remains forever in the eyes of the Father as His Delight. That is historically true and it is inwardly true.

In the context of that, the writer of Hebrews, quoting an Old Testament verse, writes in Hebrews 10:38, *"Now the just shall live by faith: but if any man draw back, my soul shall have no pleasure in him."* The just shall live by faith. That is what we have been addressing. In the Second, where we are, we live exclusively by faith. The Second is God's satisfaction. Do you understand there is no salvation for the soul unless God is satisfied? There is no New Covenant except God be fully satisfied. In fact, the coming of the New is the coming of God's satisfaction. The New has come IN Christ for the New is Christ in you! He resides in you as the satisfaction of the Father. Do you realize there is no Salvation, no New Covenant – none of that, no relationship with God except it begin upon the premise of God being perfectly and eternally satisfied? That just boggles the religious mind! The reason religion has a problem with this is because we still attempt to measure God's satisfaction in a manner in which God has and will never do so. That is how the Church can still preach an unsatisfied God. They will not admit such a thing, but that is exactly what you will hear. The Christian religion declares a God that still does not possess what He has always desired and no one knows when He will. They will speculate about it and present their timetables and charts they have charted out. However, the satisfaction of God is not determined by the passing of years and millennia. It is revealed in this tremendous statement: THIS IS MY SON IN WHOM I HAVE BEEN DELIGHTING. It was incredible for that to be spoken on a mountain two thousand years ago, but how much greater for us is it that God will and desires to make that very same declaration and divine introduction in our souls, that we may know fulfillment and satisfaction in the presence of the indwelling Christ.

In view of that, I present Hebrews 1:1-2, *"God, having of old time spoken unto the fathers in the prophets by divers portions and in divers manners, hath at the end of these days spoken unto us in (his) Son."*[20] God, who spoke in many different ways and at many different times, has spoken finally, perfectly; His concluding AMEN has come in His Son. In a sentence, let me make this as clear as possible. Either there is the promise of Christ or there is the presence of Christ. There is no other option. What I mean is either we have promises for God to fulfill, or we have the very presence of Christ living in us as the fulfillment (yes and Amen) of all promises.[21] There is no other alternative.

So again we go back to Hebrews saying the just shall live by faith, but if any man draw back, God will have no pleasure in him. To what are they drawing back? They are drawing back to what is beneath. Drawing back to the Adamic man in whom God had no pleasure, and attempting to add religious observances to the Adamic nature. God says of that man, *"My soul shall have no pleasure in him."*

---

[20] American Standard Version

[21] 2 Corinthians 1:20 For all the promises of God in him are yea, and in him Amen, unto the glory of God by us.

That displeasure is not something that starts to happen to you when you draw back. What happens is that you are relating again and finding your life in the man in whom God has never had pleasure and you are attempting to offer for acceptance that man God has already judged and put from His sight.[22] That takes "backsliding" to a whole other level, does it not? When it is all about us, backsliding is 'he has fallen off the wagon. That boy has gone crazy.' However, this is in the context of eternal reality and the writer of Hebrews writes that those who backslide, those who are drawing back to a creation and a system in which He has no pleasure, are stepping outside of predetermined boundaries, outside of which you can never have an experiential relationship with God. You may think you do, and imagine you do, but you do not! I know this is difficult to read, but it is very true. God accepts ONE relationship. God involves Himself in One relationship. The Grace of God has already brought us into that relationship. We seem always to pray in vain. We pray with a vain expectation. We say, 'God make me this, make me that, and give me the ability.' We have to turn and see our God-given state of being. God would have us, who are in Christ to know that the One who is in us, is made unto us everything that we have been praying for God to give us or to make us. That is the point. We want God to make us something instead of revealing in us what He has made His Son to be in us. How different it is when we see salvation upon perfect ground and in the context of a satisfied God.

If we are to comprehend salvation, it must begin upon the basis of a satisfied God. If you are attempting to know and experience the full reality of salvation, you cannot do it

---

[22] John 3:18 He who is believing in him is not judged, but he who is not believing hath been judged already, because he hath not believed in the name of the only begotten Son of God. – YLT

when you believe that you are dealing with a God that is just as unfulfilled and disillusioned as you are. This is why all spiritual comprehension begins and continues in the inward revealing of the Son; for in His face we behold the eternal satisfaction of God's heart, the conclusion of His will, etc. In Ephesians 1:9-10 we read about the dispensation of the fullness of times in which God has gathered and summed up all things in Christ. Paul also refers to this in Colossians 1:25, *"Whereof I am made a minister, according to the dispensation of God which is given to me for you, to fulfil the word of God."* Paul declares that his ministry is in accordance to the dispensation of the fullness of times. Do not let the word "dispensation" throw you off into the future. I have heard people who have twenty dispensations, thirty dispensations. Most say that we are in the dispensation of Grace or the Church Age. No, we are IN CHRIST. As far as God is concerned, that is the only dispensation (or administration)[23] that remains. The one administration (law and prophets) testified of Him as coming; the other (New Covenant) exists because He has come. Everything God promised, He has fulfilled in the Son, for the Son embodies and personifies the eternal satisfaction of the Father, and in view of that Son He has said, "it is good," and He has rested from all of His work. The question that comes to me is, "when do we find our rest?" When do we stop laboring

---

[23] 2 Corinthians 3:7-11
But if the ministration of death, written and engraven in stones, was glorious, so that the children of Israel could not stedfastly behold the face of Moses for the glory of his countenance; which glory was to be done away: How shall not the ministration of the Spirit be rather glorious? For if the ministration of condemnation be glory, much more doth the ministration of righteousness exceed in glory. For even that which was made glorious had no glory in this respect, by reason of the glory that excelleth. For if that which is done away was glorious, much more **that which remaineth** is glorious.

and attempting to attain what God has already given? This is the point of Paul's letters is it not? We have the Spirit of God that we might know the things that are freely given of God. About what is Paul writing? What is given? Christ! The Christ he has previously written as being made unto us righteousness, sanctification, redemption, wisdom.[24] What is freely given? We have been given Christ, who is all (all fullness, all spiritual blessing) in all.[25] That is what is freely given, and the Spirit of God works in us that we may come to the acknowledgment of Him who is made unto us all things.[26] The Spirit of God does not work in us according to unfulfilled promises God has left us, but He would reveal the Son in whom every promise is fully realized. The Spirit's work in our souls is not toward making us better Christians so we can finally satisfy God. He works in our souls according to Truth, in order to make our souls cognizant of the indwelling Son who eternally satisfies His heart. That is so we may live and walk in the Light of that One and that our souls would be transformed in the Light of

---

[24] 1 Corinthians 1:30-31
But of him are ye in Christ Jesus, who of God is made unto us wisdom, and righteousness, and sanctification, and redemption: That, according as it is written, He that glorieth, let him glory in the Lord.

1 Corinthians 2:12
Now we have received, not the Spirit of the world, but the Spirit which is of God; that we might know the things that are freely given to us of God.

[25] 2 Peter 1:3
According as his divine power hath given unto us all things that pertain unto life and godliness, through the knowledge of him that hath called us to glory and virtue:

[26] Colossians 2:2-3
That their hearts might be comforted, being knit together in love, and unto all riches of the full assurance of understanding, to the acknowledgement of the mystery of God, and of the Father, and of Christ; In whom are hid all the treasures of wisdom and knowledge.

that One.

The Church focuses so much on trying to manifest the Kingdom in the earth, yet God's desire is to get those who are in the heavens to know where they are and live daily in that realization. What we call a manifestation of the Kingdom in the earth, in the majority of cases, is nothing more than our false definitions of what it means or looks like! You see the Kingdom of God has no natural evidence. That is what Jesus says in Luke 17:20, *"The kingdom of God cometh not with observation."* The Kingdom of God does not come or appear through ocular evidence.[27] The eye cannot behold it. The Spirit of God must reveal Him within. Remember when Jesus asked, "Who do men say that I am?" He did not ask who does John or Hezekiah say that I am. He does not ask in that manner because He is summing up the understanding of mankind as a whole and does so in order to demonstrate that man's understanding (which is based upon natural observation) will always fall short of reality. It may sound impressive and even spiritual, because they were saying that Jesus was one of the prophets come back from the dead, etc. However, in all of their speculations, they did not know who He was. Man does not and cannot know.[28] The only one who could vocalize who

---

[27] NT:3907 παρατήρησις parateresis (par-at-ay'-ray-sis); from NT:3906; inspection, i.e. ocular evidence: KJV - obervation. *(Biblesoft's New Exhaustive Strong's Numbers and Concordance with Expanded Greek-Hebrew Dictionary. Copyright © 1994, 2003, 2006 Biblesoft, Inc. and International Bible Translators, Inc.)*

[28] 1 Corinthians 2:11-14
For what man knoweth the things of a man, save the Spirit of man which is in him? even so the things of God knoweth no man, but the Spirit of God. Now we have received, not the Spirit of the world, but the Spirit which is of God; that we might know the things that are freely given to us of God. Which things also we speak, not in the words which man's wisdom teacheth, but which the Holy Ghost teacheth; comparing Spiritual things with Spiritual. But the natural man receiveth not the things of the

He was, was the one to whom the Father revealed Him. Those are the only ones who will ever see the evidence of the Kingdom of God and thereby behold the object of God's own satisfaction and the full realization of His expectation. Those who live by faith are those who behold the evidence and the substance from which all natural faculties are forever shut out. What is faith? Faith is the God-given comprehension that is anchored in eternal reality, the reality that is not seen and cannot be seen by the impotent faculties of man. Faith is the seeing of Christ as the embodiment of all that was expected (under the Old Covenant) and the evidence that could not be exhibited through the agency of types and figures. Faith alone operates in Christ, for it is by faith that we behold Him as the sum of all spiritual things. If we are not inwardly beholding the Son by faith, we will continue to live in a state of dissatisfaction, for we will possess a vain expectation that looks to something other than the Son Himself as its end.

That brings us to Hebrews 2:6-11, *"But one in a certain place testified, saying, What is man, that thou art mindful of him? or the son of man, that thou visitest him? Thou madest him a little lower than the angels; thou crownedst him with glory and honour, and didst set him over the works of thy hands: Thou hast put all things in subjection under his feet. For in that he put all in subjection under him, he left nothing that is not put under him. But now we see not yet all things put under him. But..."* The writer is actually in a different way declaring not I, but Christ. He is saying we are not seeing man measuring up to that for which we think he was created. *"But we see Jesus, who was made a little lower than the angels for the suffering of death, crowned*

Spirit of God: for they are foolishness unto him: neither can he know them, because they are Spiritually discerned.

with glory and honour; that he by the grace of God should taste death for every man. For it became him, for whom are all things, and by whom are all things, in bringing many sons unto glory, to make the captain of their salvation perfect through sufferings. For both he that sanctifieth and they who are sanctified are all of one: for which cause he is not ashamed to call them brethren." It seems that most of us find ourselves seeking God upon the basis of our own dissatisfaction concerning the imperfections that we see in ourselves. We come to him asking the question: what is man? God why do you continue to work with me? Look at me! I fall so short of your glorious desire. If I were God, I would have just cast me aside long ago! Such discontentment will always be the state of our conscience while we look at our situations or ourselves in order to perceive anything that is spiritually relevant. Seek and ye shall find is a true statement, but it also must be said that the finding and knowing of spiritual reality is solely determined upon whether or not you are seeking that reality where it can be found. Are we knocking on the right Door so that God can open it unto us? It has pleased the Father that in His Son all fullness should dwell. Are we seeking fullness within those perimeters or are we seeking it elsewhere? Fullness and perfection can only be found where God has eternally determined it to dwell.

We approach God in our false understanding of incompleteness, we project onto God, our inward discontentment, which is based upon our misplaced expectation, and we convince ourselves that God is just as unhappy with us as we are. There again, we define God's view with us in view. His view is not defined by flesh and blood; God has already put that man (Adamic man, you and me) out of the picture by the death of the Cross. Here is the grace of God. By the Cross, He has brought us into union with the One unto whom He looks. That is why God remains satisfied. His perspective is not bound to the variableness of humanity, but is eternally united to Christ who abides the same.

Brother T. Austin Sparks gives a tremendous definition of the gospel. He writes, *"The gospel is the Good News of a Satisfied God."* That exploded like an atomic bomb in my heart. As I read that statement, I realized that Paul and every other writer of the New Testament declared a satisfied God by proclaiming the indwelling Christ as the sole object of His satisfaction. We must understand that Christ did not become God's satisfaction, but He came as the satisfaction of God because He is the beginning and conclusion of God's eternal plan. God has given us this Son and He is pleased to reveal this Son in us, so that our souls may experience satisfaction as God has everlastingly defined it. In Colossians 1:25, Paul writes, *"Whereof I am made a minister, according to the dispensation of God which is given to me for you, to fulfil the word of God."* Paul was a minister in accordance to this dispensation. He calls this same dispensation, "The dispensation of the fullness of times." The New Covenant is the dispensation of fulfillment. The Old Testament presents us with a dispensation of promise and prophesy; an administration of God in which He utilized external things such as days, months, years (especially seen in the feasts of Israel) to testify of a coming administration in which those times and elements would be consummated. The ministry given to Paul (and to all in whom Christ is revealed) is the declaration that the promised consummation of those times and external elements has come in Christ. Paul sums up this dispensation, this administration of fulfillment in this glorious statement: CHRIST IN YOU. That is why he can say that it was given him to fulfill the word of God. It was given to Paul to declare, with an unveiled soul, the indwelling Son, as the satisfaction of whom the entire volume of the book is written. It is important for us to understand that fulfillment was never something that had to take place at a certain time, fulfillment was Someone who was to come at the appointed time as the fullness of all times. As it is historically, it is inwardly. We will never know fulfillment and thereby know the satisfaction of the Father, until our souls are perpetually beholding the Son in whom God has reached His end (goal).

The declaring of that Son is the declaration of the fulfillment of every word of God written and spoken. (see Hebrews 1:1-2) This is why Paul says, "If any man preach another gospel (which is not another) let him be accursed." He is going back to the Old Testament and the accursed things. He is speaking of the accursed idols and the banned things that were not permitted to be brought into the camp of Israel.[29] Those things were under God's judgment. They were not something that God would judge and destroy, but something He had already judged. Paul realized that the false gospel that the Judaizers were propagating actually was causing the Galatians to bring into the camp of the "true" Israel of God,[30] that which God had accursed and eternally cast outside of the camp. Achan did the same thing and they said he had troubled Israel. What does Paul say about those preaching this "other gospel"? He says they are troubling you! They have brought the accursed thing or man into the camp and have made that man and his

---

[29] Galatians 1:6-7
I marvel that ye are so soon removed from him that called you into the grace of Christ unto another gospel: Which is not another; but there be some that trouble you, and would pervert the gospel of Christ.

[30] Galatians 6:15-16
For in Christ Jesus neither circumcision availeth anything, nor uncircumcision, but a new creature. And as many as walk according to this rule, peace be on them, and mercy, and upon the Israel of God.

betterment the object of your pursuit. That is not the gospel, for it gives the hearer or reader a false expectation. Their expectation was being deviated from the inward revelation of the true object of God's satisfaction and they were now expecting to become the object of his satisfaction through religious efforts and observation. So, what is the answer that Paul gives to us? If we are not to look at ourselves and attempt to measure up, what is the answer?

"But we see Jesus..." We look at ourselves and we think God looks at us as we do. However, there is only One unto whom He looks, for there is only One that satisfies His heart, and we will never be that One. Paul says it beautifully in Galatians 2:6 when he writes, *"the face of man God accepteth not."*[31] There is One Face that He accepts for it is that One Face in view of which He did and said all things. As we are praying, "God help me be that, help me make it, help me do that." God is saying "Turn to see the One that is and is made unto you all that you are wanting me to make you. I want to reveal HIM in you." The soul will only be transformed when God reveals His view in it. Your soul is not transformed by thinking or even believing that you have reached some state of spiritual enhancement. The seeing of Christ is not a corrective view, but a superseding view. In other words, seeing Christ does not correct us in order to make us acceptable to God. It corrects the direction and perspective of the heart that we may live with the eyes of our heart fixed upon the only One that is accepted of God. Man was never intended to be the One that pleases God. Even when such statements of pleasure were made in the scripture with men in view, it was because they were a type of the Son.

---

[31] Young's Literal Translation

"But we see Jesus" is the answer. "We see Jesus" is not a coping mechanism. It is not saying, "Well, man is a mess, and right now all we can do is just look at Jesus. Until we can finally look at man because he at last looks like Jesus." We do not look to Jesus until we can look at ourselves and see that which satisfies God. What a perverse thought. This is speaking of the perpetual gazing of our hearts upon the only One that has ever satisfied the Father, meaning the only One unto whom God has ever looked for His pleasure. God revealing Jesus Christ in our souls and Him becoming the object of our affection and the vision of our hearts is the only answer. That is spiritual understanding. It is not a tool to achieve spiritual sufficiency. Beholding Jesus IS spiritual sufficiency, because it is the beholding of Him in us as the all-sufficient One.

Christ in you is the full satisfaction of the Father. That is no more beautifully displayed than on the Day of Atonement. In the high priest, we see Jesus magnificently typified. At a point during that awesome day, the high priest went behind the veil. All of Israel stood at the door awaiting his appearing, so that they would, in his appearing, know their standing with God. They were doing something very important. They were waiting and looking with expectation. They were waiting patiently because until they saw HIM there were only questions and speculations. There was nothing but questions with regard to their relationship with God or with God being satisfied. We will deal with the importance of patience and waiting in a later chapter. The only time there are questions is when He is hidden from our view. The only time there is a question with regard to our standing, our relationship, and God's satisfaction is when He is hidden from the eyes of the soul. The fact is, until His appearing, we are the view, and it is so unstable, causing many questions to abound! In that state, we are the object, so the question is always, "Is God satisfied with us?" The problem is that the One with whom He is satisfied is hidden from your sight.

We must turn our hearts that the veil of flesh that remains upon our hearts would be removed, so that we may see our relationship with God as it is in heaven.[32] Our relationship with God as it is in heaven, does not have us as its anchor or security, for it does not have us as its means or measure. The High Priest was their relationship with God and he was standing in the Holiest of All accepted of God. God is satisfied with him. Nevertheless, only questions remained in the hearts of Israel until he came out and showed himself to them, and then in the seeing of him, when the veil was no longer an obstacle, they saw the answer to the questions. There are no more questions when he appears. There were no more questions with regard to relationship with God – He was their standing with God! There were no more questions concerning whether or not God was satisfied. Yes, standing before their eyes was the One in whom God was satisfied and because of his garments of beauty and glory they saw their union with him. While it is true that such was external back then, that exact reality must be taking place in the soul. To those who look for Him, He shall appear as the full salvation of the soul.[33] God desires to unveil our hearts to Him unto whom He looks.

---

[32] 2 Corinthians 3:16-18
Nevertheless when it shall turn to the Lord, the vail shall be taken away. Now the Lord is that Spirit: and where the Spirit of the Lord is, there is liberty. But we all, with open face beholding as in a glass the glory of the Lord, are changed into the same image from glory to glory, even as by the Spirit of the Lord.

[33] Hebrews 9:28
So Christ also, having been offered once to bear the sins of many, will appear a second time for salvation without reference to sin, to those who eagerly await Him. - NASU

Let me end this chapter by stressing the fact that we begin in the satisfaction of God. We begin upon that good and eternal ground of Christ. That is our beginning. That is why Paul can ask in Galatians, *"Having begun in the Spirit, are you now made perfect in the flesh?"* Paul understands the greatness of what they have come to because he is seeing the One in whom they are living. The satisfaction of God is our beginning, not an end we achieve. We have been made to dwell in the Person of the Beginning and the End. That is why He can be called The Satisfaction of God. He is the Beginning out from whom all things originate and He is the End in that He is the summation of it all.

You and I are by birth brought into relationship with the satisfied God, and now the work of God in us is toward us living in and experiencing the fullness of that satisfaction in the revealed presence of that Son. That is what the Spirit of God does. He works in us according to God's satisfaction, not to empower us to achieve it. So I end this chapter looking again at Hebrews 10:38-39, *"Now the just shall live by faith: but if any man draw back, my soul shall have no pleasure in him. But we are not of them who draw back unto perdition; but of them that believe to the saving of the soul."* We are those that have faith unto the saving of the soul. When we read, "the saving of the soul" in certain translations it is almost as if it is not yet done. The actual word "saving" in the Greek is defined as the experiencing of an event or a state of being that has already been acquired.[34] In other words, it speaks of our souls experiencing the satisfaction of God, and living in the daily acknowledgement of Him. Understanding begins and continues in the seeing of Christ inwardly. Therefore, the

---

[34] NT:4047 περιποίησις f: the experience of an event or state which has been acquired - 'experience, to experience.' *(from Greek-English Lexicon Based on Semantic Domain. Copyright © 1988 United Bible Societies, New York. Used by permission.)*

prayer of our hearts should always be, Lord, reveal your Son. It should not be, make me like Him, or cause me to satisfy your heart. No, that is never going to happen. Father, unveil my heart to your satisfaction who abides within, because in that unveiling the transforming begins: the work of the Spirit of Truth begins.

CHAPTER TWO

THE BASIS OF THE SPIRIT'S WORK

I began the first chapter by stating that the desire of my heart is that those who have been brought into union with Christ would come to comprehend, and thereby experience inwardly the glorious riches and reality that such a union provides. It is indeed unfortunate that our being in relationship with a God who is completely satisfied is a thought that is totally absent from the hearts of most Christians. We have been taught that God is not yet satisfied and is yet working on things because He has many things to do and many loose ends to tie together. The rhetoric of those who would propose such absurdity suggests that the work of the Cross was an incomplete work at best. That misunderstanding originates in a heart that has not seen the comprehensiveness of the indwelling Christ. I have already addressed the fact that the New Covenant would not exist if God were not fully satisfied. We would not have a New Covenant. We would still have a human priest, we would still have animals sacrificed, and the Law would still be in effect if God were not satisfied because when every thing is taken to its simplest element, you have two options. You have the promise of Him, the promise of His coming, and the promise of His presence, which the Law and the Testimony present or you have Him in His Presence. There is no other option. I realize that dispensationalists hate this, but there is definitely no third option, which means that there is no greater thing to come than the salvation that has come in the Person of the indwelling Christ.

There is nothing greater to come in the future. For us, who are in Christ, there just remains the necessity to grow up into Him and knowing Him as He is. In the last chapter, I expressed that the greatness of our salvation is never found and measured until it is measured in the revealed presence of Christ Himself. If salvation is not defined in His presence, then we, by default, will define it in our own presence. In the first chapter, I referred to the unstable view most believers have with regard to their standing with God. Such variableness is the result of a self-defined measurement of salvation. However, when standing with God is defined in the revealed presence of the One who stands before His face as His eternal satisfaction, then relationship with God has perfectly been defined and measured. In such a God-given clarity, the soul is liberated to experience the salvation that Christ is made unto it.

Sadly, because of this self-absorbed perspective, we falsely define the Work of the Spirit with ourselves in view. We look at ourselves and say, "My God, I am in terrible shape, I really do not measure up." We look at ourselves and see incompleteness, insufficiency, and inconsistency and because of that self-centered perspective, we believe that the work, or more accurately the obligation of the Spirit, is to work on us in order to get us to the place and state to which we suppose we need to arrive. The fact is that grace has brought us into the place God has desired for us. He has brought us to the expected end of which Jeremiah speaks. He has brought us into His own satisfaction. He has brought us into His own pleasure. We looked at the Mount of Transfiguration where Jesus was transfigured before them, and all the things that happened there. God spoke and said, *"This is My Beloved Son in whom I am well pleased."* Now the J.P. Greene Literal Translation reads, "This is My Son, the Beloved, in whom I have been delighting." Not just the One I am delighting in presently, but the One in whom I have been eternally delighting. That has not changed and that One lives in the soul that is born of the Spirit. This Divine declaration of the Father must resound within that soul.

Salvation did not give access to a horde of people, who would bring pleasure to God's heart if they met a multitude of stringent requirements. Salvation has brought us into the Son who fully meets all requirements because none of the requirements (of the Law) would have existed if He were not before the face of His Father as the basis of their existence. That is hard for some of us to understand. It may be easier to consider the fact that none of the words we read in the testimony, such as righteous, holy, and perfect, had reason or basis to exist and indeed could not have existed except Christ were their origin. God created those words to testify of His Son. Yet because we are ignorant of that, we go to the New Testament and we see those same words used, and we immediately want ourselves to become the measure and definition of those terms, and that was never the point! They always pointed to Christ. They even now point to Christ. Now Christ lives in us as the Essential Being and Eternal Substance of those terms. We can convince ourselves that we have reached something of reality, but the face in which that reality is being defined is either the source of truth or deception.

Recently, as I was doing a study in Philippians chapter 3, I found it interesting that this is exactly what Paul faced and experienced in his own heart. In Philippians 3:8-9, Paul states, *"Yea doubtless, and I count all things but loss for the excellency of the knowledge of Christ Jesus my Lord: for whom I have suffered the loss of all things, and do count them but dung, that I may win Christ, And be found in him, not having mine own righteousness, which is of the Law, but that which is through the faith of Christ, the righteousness which is of God by faith."* What I found fascinating was a commentary that I read concerning verse nine. The commentary[35] reads, *"as the verb εὑρίσκομαι (be found), while it has a passive termination, has an active signification, and means—to recover what you have voluntarily given up, I have not hesitated to differ from the opinion of others. For, in this way, the meaning will be more complete, and the doctrine the more ample—Paul renounced everything that he had, that he might recover them in Christ; and this corresponds better with the word gain, for it means that it was no trivial or ordinary gain, inasmuch as Christ contains everything in himself. And, unquestionably, we lose nothing when we come to Christ naked and strip of everything. For those things, which we previously imagined, on false grounds, that we possessed, we then begin really to acquire. He, accordingly, shews more fully, how great the riches of Christ are, because we obtain and find all things in him."* That is wonderful to me and it caused me to see Paul's statement, "to be found in Him" in a much more significant way. I realize that Paul is saying that his desire now is to be found and have an experiential participation in a union with Christ wherein He is made unto him all things. But this makes it even clearer. He is making known that he had found the real thing in Christ. He counted all else as dung in view of His exceeding greatness and in that Light and upon that basis, he desired to be found in Christ, not having his own righteousness, which is one that is originated and measured in self. Why? It is because in Christ he had found, eternally

---

[35] John Calvin

and perfectly defined, all of the things that he at one time had in ignorance defined in his own person. When the real came into view, the false that was based upon self and self-labor was seen to be the dung it had always been in the Light of the Son. Righteousness had now been defined as Christ in Paul and now he no longer desired to possess or attempt to acquire a "false righteousness" that is defined by his own religious labor. Once again, it must be emphasized that such a counting loss is the direct result of the inward appearing of the Christ of God. It is in the Light of His coming that we are able to relinquish our hold on what we have considered gain. In His revealed presence, there is an inward reckoning dead of what is dead, suffering the loss of what is loss and counting as dung what is dung. If we attempt to do this without first beholding reality in the face of Christ, the death and the dung will still seem to be of some residual worth. That comes to be true with every aspect of salvation. He defines and embodies it or it is not defined or embodied. Do not fool yourself into thinking that you are the embodiment of anything of spiritual reality.

I repeat, the greatness of salvation is not defined within us. I tried that for many years, and that is such is a frustrating condition. Either you are self righteous because of it, or you are condemned because of it. In both cases, the soul never sees the One that God looks upon with eternal delight. We never see the One that God sees. The Spirit of God is at all times working in our hearts that we would come to see who He sees – the satisfaction of His heart, the One who has eternally pleased Him and will eternally please Him. Salvation is our being brought into union with the Son of His satisfaction. I was looking at a progression in the scriptures concerning this thought. In Exodus 4:22 you see God, if you look at it in the Light of the fulfillment of the New Covenant, declaring a predetermined view, a predestination if you will. *"And thou shalt say unto*

Pharaoh, Thus saith the LORD, Israel is my son, even my firstborn." Notice they have not gone through the door at this point. They have not killed the lamb, they have not applied the blood of the lamb, and they have not partaken of the lamb. Nevertheless, God says Israel is My Son, even My Firstborn. This is a predetermined viewpoint. That is the predestined view of the Father.

In Exodus 12, we see them entering into the door, partaking of the lamb, and in this we see them now being brought, by the death of the lamb, into that predetermined perspective of God. We must take this back to Ephesians 1: "has predestinated us." Predestination has become such a misunderstood term because we understand that term with ourselves as the object of that term. But that word actually means to determine or mark out boundaries in advance, meaning that before anything was created, God determined the boundaries in which He would know and accept all things. So the predetermined view of the Father concerning Israel in Exodus 4 is, "Israel is My Son." Then they are brought by the blood of the lamb into that predetermined place; within the boundaries, which God had predetermined. We must understand that Israel (as a group of people) was never the object of God's point of view. God's object was always His Son. That does not change because they go into the door. Their going into the door actually fulfills God's predetermination concerning them. They enter as many, but they become One in the partaking of the death of the lamb and are brought forth as One Son raised up out from among the dead (represented by Egypt). God's view is always SON and the Cross never made God's view many, but brought the increase of the One that pleases Him. Not sons plural, but SON. That is why in Galatians Paul says not seeds, but unto THE SEED, which is CHRIST.[36] There is never in the view of the Father a plurality. There is always the singleness of His predetermination. As we grovel in our self-centeredness and dictate to God the way in which we want Him to operate in our hearts, with a self-centered view toward our betterment or our spiritual enhancement, I am so glad that we have a Christ centered God. That phrase was first brought to my attention by a good friend. It rings so true, and it causes my heart to rejoice in the solidity of our God's point of view. Even when we are self-centered and self-deceived, God remains centered upon the One that has always stood before Him as his delight.[37] His view has and will never change, His working and the basis of His work has and will never change.

We see Israel being brought into that predetermined view by the blood of the lamb. Then we see that predetermined place actually defined in Exodus 19:4. He defines where they have been brought. *"I bare you on eagles' wings, and brought you unto Myself."* The predetermination of God is defined in Union with God in Christ. Somehow, union with Christ has been taken into the future, but this scriptural progression shows us just the opposite. Unfortunately, the great majority of Christians are still waiting on that element of salvation to take place. In fact, this verse in Exodus 19 is an Old Covenant view and testimony of a New Covenant reality that Jesus would bring to fulfillment by His death, burial, and resurrection. We read John 14:2-3, *"...I go to prepare a place for you. And if I go and prepare a place for*

---

[36] Galatians 3:16
Now to Abraham and his seed were the promises made. He saith not, And to seeds, as of many; but as of one, And to thy seed, which is Christ.

[37] Proverbs 8:30
Then I (Christ, Wisdom) was by him, as one brought up with him: and I was daily his delight, rejoicing always before him.

you, I will come again, and receive you unto myself; that where I am, ye may be also." Jesus is declaring the New Covenant fulfillment of this Old Covenant type. How has He prepared that place for us? He prepared the place in which we have now been made to dwell by the Cross, the Blood of the Lamb. He is the Door after all. It is upon the basis of our being brought into such a union, into such a relationship, that the Spirit of God works, and nothing less. He does not work on inferior ground. However, salvation and the reality of our salvation must finally come to be experienced in the heart. It has to be measured and defined in the soul. It cannot merely be the acknowledged reality of the Father's heart, but it must become the God-given acknowledgement of our hearts.

This is something that I have seen when dealing with people. Many call me about these things and I realize that they believe the gospel in word and as a matter of fact, yet so many times they have merely accepted the teachings with their head, but they have not experienced it in their heart. You can give mental and intellectual acquiescence to the facts concerning salvation, but what is aggressively accepted by the brain can remain, as something not experienced by your soul. That leaves a door open for the entrance and the accumulation of many false and deceptive doctrines. Some call it eating the meat and throwing out the bones, but it is all rotten if the basis of is not the beholding of the Son. If it does not come out of a view of Christ, it is putrid, no matter how sincerely it was presented. I remember people saying with regard to some preacher, "He says good things; every now and then you hear something good." For a long time I agreed with that and thought, yes, you are right. We can listen and every now and then hear some good stuff. But what is the origin of that "good stuff"? The words may be good, but upon what are those words predicated. When I was in certain circles of theology,

I heard scriptural words and phrases such as "Christ in you, sons of God, and Kingdom of God." I was brought by the Lord to see the false object that was in view even when those true words and phrases were used. The object seemed always to be man and never Christ. There is nothing good or beneficial there. People can hear words and say, "that is a good word," but a word does not define spiritual reality. I do not care how eloquent the word or turn of phrase, it does not define or communicate spiritual reality. Only the soul transforming work of the Spirit called The Revelation of Jesus Christ does that and nothing else.

Again, the words that declare reality can be agreed to, but the soul never experience the single meaning of those words. Spiritual reality must be experienced. I am not talking about Church experiences: "Come and experience Jesus", and many Christians define that by things such as speaking in tongues or falling on the floor under the "power." There could be times where that may take place, but that is not the experience which will allow the soul to know and be established in reality. I am referring to the inward working of the Spirit that affects and touches my soul.

The intention of the work of the Spirit is for us to SEE THE LORD. Our "duty" if we may call it that, is to declare the gospel, and that is to declare the indwelling Christ, who is the fullness of all things, and direct the heart to see Him. That is it, and then the Spirit of God does the rest. We seem to disregard the Spirit in these matters. We do not allow the Spirit to do what He alone can do. We seem to think that our eloquence, our teaching, or our instruction style can get it done, but that is not going to happen. It cannot be merely intellectually agreed to, doctrinally accepted, it must be experienced. It is not primarily an emotional event, but a true encounter with divine Truth. God revealed His Son in me. We have, as Abraham (however, in spiritual fulfillment), come to the land that must be shown unto us. God spoke to Abraham saying, "go to a land I will show you."[38] The Lord appeared. The reality of the place into which we have been brought must be shown or revealed.[39] It is tremendous when you look at the term "show" in the Hebrew, because it can be defined by the cause and effect. It is defined as a seeing, an appearing, and a vision. It also means and speaks of enjoyment and experiencing something. The only way in which our soul can ever enjoy and experientially know the salvation we presently have in Christ, is that Christ appear and become the vision and sight of our souls. Our Great Salvation must be made known, in our hearts, in His revealed presence (His face) or it is not made known at all. That is the reason most have no idea how exceedingly great our salvation is and are vainly seeking that greatness in religious pursuits or even future events. My point is, regardless of how adamant we are in our agreement with the true words; it has to be experienced inwardly.

---

[38] Genesis 12:1

[39] OT:7200 רָאָה ra'ah (raw-aw'); a primitive root; to see, literally or figuratively (in numerous applications, direct and implied, transitive, intransitive and causative): KJV – advise self, appear, approve, behold, certainly, consider, discern, (make to) enjoy, have experience, gaze, take heed, indeed, joyfully, lo, look (on, one another, one on another, one upon another, out, up, upon), mark, meet, be near, perceive, present, provide, regard, (have) respect, (fore-, cause to, let) see (-r, -m, one another), shew (self), sight of others, (e-) spy, stare, surely, think, view, visions. *(Biblesoft's New Exhaustive Strong's Numbers and Concordance with Expanded Greek-Hebrew Dictionary. Copyright © 1994, 2003, 2006 Biblesoft, Inc. and International Bible Translators, Inc.)*

I was reading a book entitled, "The Indwelling Christ" by Harmon Baldwin[40] and he gives a very simple illustration of this very thing. He writes, *"Spiritual Truth can only be learned by experience."* His comments are upon the premise of the Indwelling Christ and Christ being made unto the soul all things. Truth can only be comprehended by experience. He then gives this illustration. He writes, *"I have often seen pictures of a certain variety of a peach, but now for the first time I see one. But if I desire to know its flavor, I must taste it for myself."* How profoundly uncomplicated is that statement. *"Taste and see that the Lord is good."* The inward apprehension of salvation demands the soul's participation. You cannot just intellectually digest books about it (not even the Bible) and consequently know salvation as it is in Christ. How many of us can say that we are beholding that grand object in view of whom there is nothing worthy to compare? None of my thoughts, none of my theological ideas, none of my previous concepts are worthy of comparison because I have seen HIM! I have seen the object of contrast who supersedes everything I have ever thought.

Mr. Baldwin goes on and writes, *"After I have tasted for myself, I cannot impart my knowledge to any one else."* Notice, He is speaking as one who has experienced the taste of the peach, not the dogmatic information about it, but the taste of it; he has had a participation with that peach. That relates to the word "know" that Paul uses so many times in his epistles. It speaks of *"a full participation between the one knowing and the person or object being known."*[41] In

---

[40] Published by The Free Methodist Publishing House (1912). Noted reference on page 31

[41] NT:1921
Sometimes epiginosko implies a special participation in the object "known," and gives greater weight to what is stated; thus in John 8:32, "ye

our hearts, it does not merely speak of information that is conveyed by external means, but an inward participation and perpetual communion with the One who is revealed in us by the Father. John 8:32, *"And ye shall know the truth, and the truth shall make you free."* That word "know" is used in this verse and that is extremely important. Knowing the Truth is not the acquisition of information, but it is participation with the Truth Himself. That inward participation with the Truth is the only thing that is capable of transforming the soul of the believer. I love the fact that he stresses the absolute inability for even one who has "tasted and seen," to ever impart that reality into someone else. That seems to be our concept. We seem to think that we can communicate the reality into the souls of people. Many think that we can exhibit spiritual reality through what we do, by how much we love, or even the external activities in which we involve ourselves. That is not the case. If you are experiencing salvation, that experience is due to the work of the Spirit wherein Christ is revealed in your soul. In His revealed presence, you are experiencing Him, yet you cannot make that experience anyone else's. Each soul must know reality for itself and that necessitates that soul's submission in absolute dependence upon the Spirit of Truth, that He may make known in us the reality that only He knows. That is the direction that we must give to a heart that desires to know and experience the greatness of salvation. Information becomes a detriment if it does not also give direction. In other words, speaking about and describing the aspects of a perfect salvation is of no effectual consequence if it is not coupled with directing the heart of the hearer to turn his heart so that the Spirit of God may make known the eternal and essential substance that the words could merely illustrate. The Christian world is

---

shall know the truth." *(from Vine's Expository Dictionary of Biblical Words, Copyright © 1985, Thomas Nelson Publishers.)*

overloaded with instruction and steps for spiritual achievement. However, most have never been directed to turn their hearts unto the Father that He may unveil their hearts to see and know the Great Salvation embodied in the indwelling Christ.

There is a difference and that difference means either they are properly postured so that the Lord may make known reality or they are content with accumulating information concerning salvation and remain lost in their own illusions and the vanity of their own mind. In the previous quote, Mr. Baldwin wrote, *"An entire book might be filled with dogmatic truth concerning the peach and an entire page devoted to the explanation of its taste, but after all has been said, those who have never tasted, will not understand."* Those who are in Christ should always direct hearts unto the seeing of the Lord, so that they may experience divine reality. We should never be content merely to convince them of a doctrine to the extent that they think they understand it. 'We do not want them going away and saying, "I have that now, I understand that now, now I can move on to something more". You do not know or understand at all until you taste and see. If you are tasting and are seeing the Lord, you realize there is nothing more to move on toward, there is only the greatness and comprehensiveness of His Person to discover. May we never substitute our agreement with or belief in spiritual reality for the inward, soul transforming experiencing of the person of spiritual reality!

That is what we observe in the heart of Paul when we read his statement, "God revealed His Son in me." Paul did not exchange a lesser doctrine for a better doctrine. His soul came, by an ongoing work of the Spirit, to behold the spiritual meaning, origin, and substance of everything that his soul awaited while under that system of testimony. The expectation of his heart was fulfilled the moment he saw Christ, and the subsequent moments thereafter. I call it a perpetual moment of clarity. It never ends if the direction and expectation of our souls never ceases to be His coming. Paul continued in the beholding of the Lord and it must be that way with us. We cannot see, walk away, and say, "I have seen the Lord, now let us proceed on to something else." When you have experienced the revelation of Jesus Christ, the occupation and aspiration of your heart will be to continue in the seeing of Him. That is because you will understand that there is nothing else but Him. Now your soul is coming to experience satisfaction in the revealed presence of the One who has eternally satisfied God's heart. There is nothing else in His view and the Work of the Spirit in our hearts is toward the seeing of that Son unto whom God looks. We are brought into a living union with the Son of God's eternal satisfaction and, by that union, the Son is made unto us all that He is before the face of His Father. It is solely upon that basis that the Spirit of God works in our hearts.

His work in our hearts is predicated upon that union. We think He works upon the premise of our insufficiencies and shortcomings. It is indeed wonderful to know that God does not define salvation or measure salvation by looking at man. It took me a long time to understand that. When I make a statement like that, without fail someone will accuse me of believing that when we are saved, we can live anyway we want. That is false. I am saying that we have no life of our own to live. I am saying that the only Life we have is the One God has given in and as His Son. Moreover, if you are found outside of the confines of that Life, as far as God is concerned you do not exist! The only means of acceptance with God is to abide in and live by the Life that He has given. The Life the Son is in you is that accepted Life, for it is the Living Son who has always satisfied the Father's heart. That is true. In my mind, I believe that God knows the absolute depravity of man; therefore, I do not believe that it catches God off guard when man acts like man. I think the true offence to the Spirit of God, is when man attempts to be and imitate what only Christ is.

Remember when God spoke to Samuel about going to Jesse's house. First, we must see what actually led up to that moment. God had spoken to Saul and told him and the army of Israel to go into Amalek and destroy everything. God did not want them to leave one thing alive. Everything that had breath in it had to be destroyed. In other words, God is saying, "I want **nothing to remain but Israel**." Here is what happens next. 1Samuel 15:13, *"And Samuel came to Saul: and Saul said unto him, Blessed be thou of the LORD: **I have performed the commandment** of the LORD."* "I" have performed it. That is what the carnal mind thinks, I have performed, I have done it, I have performed what God has commanded, and I have achieved the demands of the Lord.

1 Samuel 15:14, *"And Samuel said, What meaneth then this bleating of the sheep in mine ears, and the lowing of the oxen which I hear?"* Samuel says, wait a minute. You have remaining with you that which does not remain in the sight of God. This also is reminiscent of the time in Joshua when they brought the accursed thing into the camp. We have already dealt with that, so I will not elaborate. So Samuel says why are the sheep and oxen still alive and with you? God said all of it must be put away. Now, listen to the religious mind of man. 1Samuel 15:15, *"And Saul said, They have brought them from the Amalekites: for the people **spared the best** of the sheep and of the oxen, **to sacrifice unto the LORD thy God**; and <u>the rest</u> we have utterly destroyed."* It says in Verse 9, *"But Saul and the people*

spared Agag, and **the best of** the sheep, and of the oxen, and of the fatlings, and the lambs, and **all that was good**, and would not utterly destroy them: but every thing that was **vile and refuse**, that they destroyed utterly." In whose sight is vile and refuse defined? In whose sight was the best and the good defined? Who gave them the discernment to decide what of that city was good and what of that city was evil? God said all of it was to be destroyed. All of it was refuse; all of it was vile in God's sight. God only wants Israel to remain. We do the same thing. We say to God, "I brought you the best; my best efforts, my best deeds, my best religious observances." Paul believed that every one of his efforts under the Law was accepted by God, but it was not until He saw the Accepted One that he realized **everything** he had attempted to offer to God was vile, filthy, and abominable. It is in that realization that Paul can call it all dung. That dung is everything that was identified and defined in him. That is why the satisfaction of the Father is inseparably bound to the Cross of Christ. It is in that Cross where all in which the Father found no pleasure is put away (Adam, Law, etc.) and the One who is the eternal satisfaction and pleasure of the Father is brought forth as the fullness of His eternal will. Man is that vile and abominable thing and he cannot be brought into the camp of the Israel of God. In other words, what God has already put away from His sight, must be put away from ours. However, that is not something we can do of our own. Such a putting away only takes place when our hearts are seeing the only One who pleases and eternally satisfies His soul. Nothing else could ever and can never please God. Isaiah 64:6, "…all our righteousnesses are as filthy rags…" Notice the plurality of the word righteousness. All our righteousnesses are filthy. Man attempts to define righteousness by the multiplicity of his activities and observances. God defines it in One Son. How great the grace of God that has permitted that Son to live in us and be made unto us that One Righteousness which satisfies God's heart. The work of the Spirit in us is not to refine our "righteousnesses," but to unveil our souls to the One righteous Son who abides within.

The theme of most of our prayers seems to be for God to save the best of us and use it for His glory. However, I hope you will not immediately close the book when I say, there is no best of us. That is not my opinion, Paul himself says, *"For I know that in me (that is, in my flesh,) dwelleth no good thing..."*[42] We must realize that Paul is not, in the parenthetical portion of this statement, discounting the statement "in me." In other words, Paul is not differentiating between him and his flesh. Many teach that our flesh is the bad part of us and then there is the good and spiritual part of us. Paul says IN ME (the whole of me) nothing good is found. He is further describing the in me with the phrase in my flesh. The work of God is not to put away the bad of us and to keep and cultivate the good of us. That is why the answer for Paul and the answer for us is always found in the Life of another and not the betterment and spiritual endowment of our own. The Cross brought the best, the worst, the whole of us to death. The grace of God is not toward our attaining the attributes that God considers good and pleasing. Grace is our souls being permitted to partake of and be indwelt by the only "Good Thing" that God has ever accepted and found to be His pleasure. When Paul wrote of the "good" that he desired to do in Romans 7, he was referencing the "good" of which the Law of Moses spoke and which it demanded. He realized that in spite of the multitude of his observances, he did not have, in his being and nature, the capacity to be or do the "good" for which it called. The good for which it called, was not Paul, but Christ. That is his meaning when he cries out "in me

---

[42] Romans 7:18

dwelleth no good thing." The good which God desires is not within my capacity; it is not who I am, it is only who Christ is. The wonderful news is that the Good Thing of which the Law spoke now dwells in us.

Moreover, the Spirit of God works in us upon the sure and sound basis of Christ's indwelling. The Spirit of God works upon one premise, *"In view of the fact that you are risen with Christ."*[43] However, that must also be the premise from which we seek Him. In view of the fact of that union, Paul goes on to say, *"seek those things which are above, where Christ sitteth on the right hand of God. Set your affection on things above, not on things on the earth."* Understand, this is not seeking God based upon an unfulfilled condition, but in accordance to a fulfilled condition and state of being into which we have been brought. Seeking what is above is not seeking for something we do not already have, but seeking in view of that union wherein Christ is made unto us all things; wherein Christ is made unto us that good and perfect gift that has come from above. Paul is speaking about seeking with a view to inwardly apprehend and lay hold of what God has freely given in Christ. That is only possible when "Christ our Life appears."

We cannot seek Him from a standpoint of our imperfections, requesting Him to repair our deficiencies. His desire is to reveal and make known the Perfect One in us. The Spirit of God works solely in accordance to a Finished Work, but His work in our hearts is either permitted or hindered by the posture of our souls. Again, it is not a matter of questioning the salvation of the soul. It is a matter of whether the soul is experiencing the salvation

---

[43] Colossians 3:1-4

Christ is in it. The experiencing and knowing of our current, God-given state of being (union with Christ) and all that it means, necessitates our souls being brought to the awareness of His indwelling presence. The experiencing of the indwelling Christ necessitates our seeking of Him in accordance with the fact that we are risen with or are in union with Him. When the soul is in that posture, the Spirit of God has the opening to guide it into and cause it to participate in a heavenly reality which union has already provided. It is always that way. When our hearts are set in the proper direction, the Spirit of God will bring about the result, which is the appearing of Christ in us. In the light of that appearing, we are made to know what has been the condition of our souls since the moment of being born of the Spirit of God. *"Whenever Christ our life is revealed, then also you will be revealed with Him in glory."*[44] First, notice the literal rendering of this verse. It begins with the very significant term "whenever." Not when, but whenever. This is important because it takes the revealing or appearing of Christ outside of the realm of times and events, making it truly a matter of the posture of the heart that is seeking and looking for His appearing. Paul means that when our hearts are turned and seek within the context of a present reality, then as a consequence of that condition, the Lord will appear. That is why it is "whenever." The appearing of the Lord in our hearts is a matter of the orientation of our souls and nothing else. When Christ our Life does appear what is it that takes place? Well, simply nothing takes place that is not already taking place in us by the indwelling of Christ. The meaning of the word appearing in the verse under consideration actually means to render apparent.[45] It does

---

[44] J.P. Green Literal Version

[45] NT:5319 φανερόω phaneroo (fan-er-o'-o); from NT:5318; to render apparent (literally or figuratively): KJV - appear, manifestly declare,

not imply the making real of something, but rendering apparent and openly displaying that which is real. That is what takes place in our hearts, when Christ our Life is revealed. The reality that He is in us and is made unto us is made apparent to the soul that has been made a partaker of His divine nature. In that revealing, our union with Him will be seen as a reality and that will further confine the seeking and searching of our hearts within the divine perimeters of union. This will allow the Spirit to continue to disclose the full dimensions of this Great Salvation we have in Christ.

God desires to show us a salvation that is "without sin." Hebrews 9:28, *"So Christ also, having been offered once to bear the sins of many, shall appear a second time for salvation without reference to sin, to those who eagerly await Him."*[46] Just as with Colossians chapter 3, this does not refer to an external appearing of the Lord and it speaks to the posture of the soul. This verse beautifully speaks of the revealing of Christ in the soul as the full and complete satisfaction of the Father's heart. Remember, this letter to the Hebrews was entirely with reference to their being carried on, by the Spirit of Truth, into the Eternal Substance unto which the shadows of the Old Covenant system pointed. It is not for them to come to the New as their state of being, but for their souls to come to the acknowledgment of their state of being. In keeping with the context of this letter, this verse has absolutely nothing to do with future happenings and events. It has to do with a soul seeking and God revealing a full and complete salvation that is embodied in Christ. This speaks of Christ appearing in the soul as the personification of the Law's righteous demands,

---

(make) manifest (forth), shew (self). *(Vine's Expository Dictionary of Biblical Words, Copyright © 1985, Thomas Nelson Publishers.)*

[46] New American Standard

thus showing Himself mightily within us as our Great Salvation, which has no flaws and does not lack anything concerning completeness as did the Law.

"Without sin" refers to the fact that Christ's appearing in us has no reference to sin, for it is not as the Law, which could not bring the comers unto perfection. On the contrary, the appearing of Christ in our souls is the coming of the perfection of which the Law spoke; it is the coming of the One who has fully satisfied the will and intention of the Father and has brought the system of shadows to its intended fulfillment. Therefore, God does not now relate to us by the Law as those who fall short of the Glory of God, but He reveals the One who is the Glory of God within. It is that One for which we are to look. It is that One unto whom the affection of our souls must be set. He shall appear as the salvation, which does not have man and his falling short as a point of reference at all.

If that is the determined orientation of our hearts, Christ will appear as the Second. If you search this in the Interlinear Bible, you will notice that "time" is not in the verse at all. The reason is that it does not refer to a time or event that will happen at a certain moment. Christ's appearing in your soul is inseparably related to the direction of your soul's affection. To those who look for HIM, shall HE appear as the Second. He does not come with reference to the first, which brought God's heart no pleasure in that it could not fulfill His purpose. Christ appears in our souls as the Second. What is the Second? Well, you will have to refer to Hebrews chapter 10 for the answer to that, but the Second is, in its fullest definition, the Risen Christ living in our hearts as the full and eternal satisfaction of the Father.[47] The Second is Christ in you, the One concerning whom the volume of the book was written. The revelation of Christ is God unveiling our souls to our full and perfect salvation (the Second), personified in the indwelling Son.

I have already addressed this when I discussed Hebrews chapter 2, but God never gives man the ability or capacity to please Him. People who have themselves in view pray with that intention and always seem to want God to correct their defectiveness. However, the answer for the soul is always: BUT WE SEE JESUS. That is not a corrective view. It is not a view toward the betterment of the one that falls short. It is a superseding view; a God-given vision, which overrides and overrules all that falls short. God has, by the Cross, put away that poor and wretched man that we are (by natural birth). That man is not the perspective of God. God does not look to the Adamic man to find His heart's delight or the fulfillment of His will. His Son is His vision and it is upon that Son He has eternally set His gaze. The Spirit of God works in us toward the same end. That

---

[47] Hebrews 10:1-9
For the Law, since it has only a shadow of the good things to come and not the very form of things, can never by the same sacrifices year by year, which they offer continually, make perfect those who draw near. Otherwise, would they not have ceased to be offered, because the worshipers, having once been cleansed, would no longer have had consciousness of sins? But in those sacrifices there is a reminder of sins year by year. For it is impossible for the blood of bulls and goats to take away sins. Therefore, when He comes into the world, He says, "Sacrifice and offering Thou hast not desired, But a body Thou hast prepared for Me; In whole burnt offerings and sacrifices for sin Thou hast taken no pleasure. "Then I said, 'Behold, I have come (In the roll of the book it is written of Me) To do Thy will, O God.'" After saying above, "Sacrifices and offerings and whole burnt offerings and sacrifices for sin Thou hast not desired, nor hast Thou taken pleasure in them" (which are offered according to the Law), then He said, "Behold, I have come to do Thy will." He takes away the first in order to establish the second. - NASB

the man God has put away is no longer the scope of our soul's vision. He would lift our gaze into heaven itself to behold the Son, which God beholds and of whom He declares, "It is good." I want us to see this very clearly. The Spirit does not work in us in view of our imperfections, in order to correct our faults and shortcomings. We have already stated that the Spirit of the Truth will only work in accordance with and upon the ground of the Truth. Now, if that is true, then the work of the Spirit is to bring the soul to the acknowledgment of the Truth and in that acknowledgment, the soul is made free. From what is the soul made free? SELF! In the revealed presence of the Truth Himself, the soul is made free from the veil of flesh that has kept it ignorant of the salvation Christ is made unto it, by making man the object by which it attempts to define and measure spiritual reality. The revealing of the Son takes away the veil (upon the heart) that has kept the pleasure and satisfaction of God's heart hidden from the soul's view. Without that God-given perspective, we are the automatic and default point of reference. In that condition, all aspects of our salvation are falsely measured and defined in the face of the wrong man.

Matthew chapter 5 will help to illustrate my point. First, we must notice in verse 17, Jesus says, *"Think not that I am come to destroy the Law, or the prophets: I am not come to destroy, but to fulfil."* Remember we have been addressing the righteousness of which the Law spoke being fulfilled in us through our union with Christ and the Spirit of God working in our souls to awaken us to the righteousness of God that is measured and defined in another and not ourselves. So, it is important that I preface what I am about to write, as Jesus did, with these words. He did not come to destroy the Law and prophets. Jesus came as the fulfillment of that perfect testimony and as the conclusion of that glorious expectation. Jesus did not come declaring the invalidity of the Law. He came as the eternal validation of the Law; He came as the satisfaction and realization of it. With that being established, He begins to speak to them concerning a righteousness that "exceeds that of the scribes and the Pharisees." Matthew 5:20, *"For I say unto you, That except your righteousness shall exceed the righteousness of the scribes and Pharisees, ye shall in no case enter into the kingdom of heaven."* On the surface, that seems like such a difficult task. It seems impossible when you consider the disciplined lifestyle of these devout scribes and Pharisees. Things such as the memorization of the entire Torah and asceticism were just part of their external "evidences" of righteousness. However, Jesus is speaking concerning a righteousness that exceeds and supersedes their "external" righteousness. Jesus goes on to say, *"Ye have heard that it was said by them of old time, Thou shalt not kill; and whosoever shall kill shall be in danger of the judgment: But I say unto you, That whosoever is angry with his brother without a cause shall be in danger of the judgment: and whosoever shall say to his brother, Raca, shall be in danger of the council: but whosoever shall say, Thou fool, shall be in danger of hell fire."*[48] He continues by saying, *"Ye have heard that it was said by them of old time, Thou shalt not commit adultery: But I say unto you, That whosoever looketh on a woman to lust after her hath committed adultery with her already in his heart."* [49] So many have looked at these words and thrown their hands up in utter frustration, falsely believing that Jesus is giving a more stringent "instruction to men" than the Law of Moses. Remember again, Jesus is speaking of an "exceeding righteousness." Many will think that Jesus is not only restricting the activities of the body, but He is now

---

[48] Matthew 5:21-22

[49] Matthew 5:27-28

necessitating the cessation of the thought of the action. Now, that is such a condemning thought when attempting to define and measure this "exceeding righteousness" by man (even the best most devout man). He is not describing a more rigorous external Law. Actually, He is describing the intention of the Law itself. The Law was never to be a means for man to attain righteousness; it was to bring us to the Righteousness of God Himself. The righteousness that satisfies the Law and therefore which satisfies God, is not the righteousness that is assumed due to exercise and observance. Righteousness is given to us as the Life and Being of Christ Himself. Jesus is making known the spiritual intention of the Law and He is showing Himself to be the fulfillment of that intention. The Law of Moses was never the means of flesh acquiring righteousness. It was a testimony of the Righteous One. It is important to understand that the Law was not meant to bring us to Christ-likeness, but to bring us to Christ. It was intended to bring us to the One who fulfilled to the fullest degree every demand and satisfied every obligation.[50]

Paul was a Pharisee and possessed the "righteousness of the Pharisees," which Jesus here addresses. As we have stated, one thing brought about the transition from the righteousness of the Pharisees to the righteousness that exceeds in his heart: "God revealed His Son in me". At this point, I think it is fitting to explore what I, at one time, considered as contradictions in Paul's letters. First, we have Philippians 3:6, *"...Touching the righteousness which is in the Law, blameless."* Second, we read in Romans 7:18-21, *"For I know that in me (that is, in my flesh,) dwelleth no good thing: for to will is present with me; but how to*

---

[50] Galatians 3:24
Wherefore the Law was our schoolmaster to bring us unto Christ, that we might be justified by faith.

perform that which is good I find not. For the good that I would I do not: but the evil which I would not, that I do. Now if I do that I would not, it is no more I that do it, but sin that dwelleth in me. I find then a Law, that, when I would do good, evil is present with me." There is much here that could occupy our time, but I want to concentrate on this seeming contradiction. I have a reason for this. Paul says in Philippians that he was blameless touching the righteousness "in the Law." In Romans, he says that when attempting to do good, evil is always present and he is incapable of doing the good he seeks. Now, again we have to keep in mind that when he speaks of doing "the good," he is speaking of "the good" which the Law required. To some these two statements could be construed as being in disagreement. They are not at all. In Philippians, Paul is writing with regard to the "observances of the Law." When addressing the exercise and observance of the ordinances of the Law, Paul was blameless in their execution and performance. Yet, in Romans, Paul is not referring to the observance of the Law's rituals, but the fulfilling of its intention. Paul came to see that, regardless of his undying zeal and wholehearted ambition to perform the actions the Law prescribed, he was impotent to fulfill its intention and objective. The Law was not looking at Paul for its fullness and every time Paul would attempt to be that, he was confronted with the fact that he was not and could not be **WHO** it demanded. The Law, in its intention, did not make demands on and seek fulfillment from the flesh of men. It testified of the Spirit of Life. It declared and pointed toward the Perfect Man. Therefore, we must conclude that the righteousness that "exceeds" the righteousness of the Pharisees is not another "externally observed or evidenced" righteousness, but is the Righteousness, which is Spirit and Truth, which must be revealed and made known in our souls by the Spirit. This means that the Spirit of God does not work in us to assist us in the acquisition of spiritual attributes such as righteousness. He does not assist us to go up to heaven to bring it down or go to the depths to bring it up; He reveals the righteousness that is nigh even in our hearts.[51] His work in us is to unveil our hearts to the indwelling essential being of righteousness.

It is in the Light of such an unveiling that Paul can say in Philippians 3:9, *"And be found in him, not having mine own righteousness, which is of the Law, but that which is through the faith of Christ, the righteousness which is of God by faith."* The righteousness that he could never attain was now seen to be found and embodied in the indwelling Son of God. Paul was and continued to behold the righteousness that exceeded that of the scribes and Pharisees. God had revealed the righteousness that far exceeded the external observations of men. God revealed the righteousness, which is not measured or defined in man or his activities. Paul is saying, "I have counted this 'assumed righteousness' as loss and dung in the revealed light of the exceeding righteousness that Christ is in me. I see righteousness eternally measured and defined and I am not the object by which it is defined or measured. Now my earnest desire is to be found in Him not having mine own righteousness (defined by myself) which is by Law (the Pharisees' righteousness), but the righteousness that is by faith." Paul had been brought, in his heart, from the external Law of Moses to the indwelling Law of the Spirit of Life. You see, the Law of Moses demanded "another Life"; it demanded the Life that satisfies God. However, the Law of

---

[51] Romans 10:6-8
But the righteousness which is of faith speaketh on this wise, Say not in thine heart, Who shall ascend into heaven? (that is, to bring Christ down from above:) Or, Who shall descend into the deep? (that is, to bring up Christ again from the dead.) But what saith it? The word is nigh thee, even in thy mouth, and in thy heart: that is, the word of faith, which we preach.

the Spirit of Life provides the Life that the Law demanded but could not provide. In Galatians 3:21, Paul says, *"For if there had been a Law given which could have given life, verily righteousness should have been by the Law."* Notice what Paul does in this verse. He equates Life and Righteousness. He makes righteousness the automatic consequence of Life. This is not a better natural life, but the Life of the Spirit of Christ living and being in us all that He is. Righteousness is the present state and condition of a soul in relationship with the Life given of God. Righteousness is not the result of Laws kept or deeds done. Righteousness is participation with the Life of the Son that God has given. Everything of spiritual life, everything of spiritual reality is given to us through relationship, through our union with Christ.

Righteousness, or any other aspect of salvation, never becomes possessively our own. Paul was troubled concerning the Jews because of that very thing. He says, *"For being ignorant of God's righteousness, and seeking to establish their own, they did not subject themselves to the righteousness of God."*[52] "Their own" in the Greek, means one's own private and personal possession.[53] The context of this verse speaks of a righteousness, which pertains to self and is attained in a state of separation from Christ. That is how most people think of righteousness; it is their own personal and private righteousness achieved through their own religious observances. Religion today puts that

---

[52] Romans 10:3 ASV

[53] NT:2398 ἴδιος idios (id'-ee-os); of uncertain affinity; **pertaining to self**, i.e. one's own; by implication, private or **separate**: KJV - his acquaintance, when they were alone, apart, aside, due, his (own, proper, several), home, (her, our, thine, your) own (business), private (-ly), proper, severally, their (own). *(New Exhaustive Strong's Numbers and Concordance with Expanded Greek-Hebrew Dictionary. Copyright © 1994, 2003, 2006 Biblesoft, Inc. and International Bible Translators, Inc.)*

definition of righteousness as the goal toward which we are to move. That understanding is due to an abounding ignorance of the righteousness that is of God by faith.

Do not be offended with the use of the word "ignorant." It is not the same as stupid. Ignorance is a state of unawareness. It means many are unaware of the reality. It is not that they are too stupid to see it or know it, but they are unaware of the presence of what is real and therefore attempt to add what they feel to be lacking. Most believers today fall into this category. They have no idea that we begin in God's End. We begin in the One who satisfies the Father. That is where we begin; that is where God has brought us. We begin with a satisfied God. Salvation does not make it our obligation to work enough to satisfy God. We begin in the Son of His satisfaction; that is Salvation. The Work of the Spirit is upon that premise, because the Work of the Spirit is always to bring our souls into an encounter and participation with Him who is satisfied. The Spirit works in us so that we may know Christ as everything that we, in our unawareness and ignorance, have attempted to be or become.

I recently came across these statements in the *Exegetical Dictionary of the New Testament*. These statements are with regard to righteousness. They speak of righteousness as not being an accomplishment or achievement on our part, but a relationship that we must comprehend and acknowledge by seeing Him in whom we live. These comments should take your mind back to my previous statement that **salvation is our souls being permitted into a participation with a satisfied God by union with His Son wherein His Son is made unto us all that He is unto the Father**. I must repeat that is where we begin. I love that thought – we begin there. We do not get there by achievements. We begin in this union, and then God says to our souls, *"Lift up now thine* *eyes from whence you are look and walk here"*[54]; *"As ye have therefore received Christ Jesus the Lord, so walk ye in him: Rooted and built up in him, and stablished in the faith."*[55]

Unfortunately, the Righteousness that most of us seek is a righteousness that can be observed in the natural world and that can be seen with the natural eyes. However, the righteousness that we must see is the righteousness that is observed only by faith. Again, faith is that God-given faculty that beholds what is unobservable to the natural eye and unknowable to the natural mind. Faith beholds Christ as the righteousness of God. Faith sees the Truth, and the Spirit of God exclusively works upon the basis of the Truth. He is called The Spirit of Truth. He does not work upon any lesser basis than The Truth Himself. Even the Greek definition of "Truth" is the appearance and essence that lies at or as the basis of a matter. [56] The Truth is the essence or presence that is the basis of something's existence. That "something" has no basis to exist except the Truth be its basis.

Before Paul came to behold the righteousness that exceeds in the revealed presence of Jesus Christ, he would read the word "righteousness" in the Old Testament scripture with himself in view and he would attempt to define that "spiritual term" by himself when that term never had him as its defining object. In other words, Paul tried to define it in

---

[54] Genesis 13:14

[55] Colossians 2:6-7

[56] NT:225 aletheia (ἀλήθεια, NT:225), "truth," is used (a) objectively, signifying "the reality lying at the basis of an appearance; the manifested, veritable essence of a matter" *(Vine's Expository Dictionary of Biblical Words, Copyright © 1985, Thomas Nelson Publishers.)*

himself because he had not seen the Truth, because the revealing of the Truth brings the essential being of that spiritual aspect into view. Righteousness, in that light, can be properly defined in the face of the One who was the basis of that term. Even when a spiritual term was applied to man, it was used exclusively as a testimony of that One Son. That is true. In view of that, how is it that we can now go to the New Testament, read those same terms, and believe that they are now speaking of us? Now, we imagine that those terms declare what we can become or what we can exhibit to others. That is why Paul says that Christ is made unto us righteousness, etc. It is not what we become, but always who He is in us and is unto us as our Life, the Life that the Law could not provide.

This brings us back to our commentary from the *Exegetical Dictionary of the New Testament*.[57] This commentary is concerning righteousness; however, it is applicable to any term declaring spiritual reality. It reads, *"For the elevation of the basic meaning of δικαιοσύνη 'righteousness' in the NT, it follows that the meaning of the word 'righteousness' as a concept of relationship, which was shaped in a peculiar way in the OT and Jewish tradition,* **is to be given precedence over** *the Greek meaning of 'righteousness' as a category within the teaching about virtue."* I love that statement. Righteousness as a concept of relationship, which was seen in a peculiar way in the Old Testament (especially with Israel), as a relationship, is to be given precedence over the Greek meaning of righteousness which is a category within the teachings about virtue (human virtue – oxymoron indeed).

---

[57] Exegetical Dictionary of the New Testament © 1990 by William B. Eerdmans Publishing Company. All rights reserved.

Religion teaches us that righteousness is achievable by understanding the teachings of virtue, the teachings of moral codes and conduct. Most concentrate on teaching and studying how to live and how to be zealous in our duties and religious observances. Religion will instruct us in ethical mannerisms and religious customs. The belief seems to be that righteousness is the result of strict adherence to those codes and customs. The familiar statement would be, "Look at that man, he prays, he attends services, he gives money, he feeds the hungry, therefore, he is a righteous man." Do you see what such an earth bound perspective and definition of righteousness produces? It directs the heart of the Christian to false evidence. It diverts the soul from the righteousness of God, which is found within the confines of our present union with Christ, unto an assumed righteousness that is achieved by man. According to the statement above, righteousness is the condition of the soul in union with the indwelling Christ. The commentary goes on and reads, *"Paul is now able to affirm such 'rightness' because of the knowledge granted to him* (the knowledge that came by the revelation of the Son), *of the one who 'lives by faith in the Son of God, who loved me and gave himself for me'*. Notice that it says that Paul is able to affirm the rightness of the believer by this God given comprehension, *"I am crucified with Christ, nevertheless I live, yet not I, but Christ liveth in me."*[58] That is how he can affirm right standing with God. He can be certain that the righteousness of the believer is acceptable because the righteousness we have as believers is not ours at all, but is Christ who lives in us. It is all contingent upon this union of our souls with the Spirit of Christ. Righteousness and any other aspect of spiritual reality is always defined and

---

[58] Galatians 2:20
I am crucified with Christ: nevertheless I live; yet not I, but Christ liveth in me: and the life which I now live in the flesh I live by the faith of the Son of God, who loved me, and gave himself for me.

measured by who He is in us and never by what we have achieved. It is never what He has given us as our own possession; He is made unto us everything that we can never be or do. The Spirit of Truth works in us upon that perfect premise of union, in order that our souls would come to comprehend the satisfaction and pleasure of God not in ourselves, but in and as Christ who lives within.

The commentary reads on and I really like this part. *"The righteousness, which determines and interweaves the life of the Christian, is **neither expected from nor produced by the Law** and the fulfillment of its demands as in the Judaism described by Paul."* Judaism said the Law looked at man in expectation for and gave man the means to produce the righteousness that was acceptable to God. However, the Law (in its intention) never expected righteousness to be achieved by man. The Law did not have man's righteousness as its expectation, but the coming of the Seed and Branch of Righteousness who was the eternal basis of its demands. This is why this commentary ends this statement with, *"it is a gift from the loving sacrifice of Jesus in his death."* This is the same as saying, *"For by grace are ye saved through faith; and that not of yourselves: it is the gift of God: Not of works, lest any man should boast."* [59] The Cross made possible that we may partake of this gift of Grace, wherein Christ lives in us and is made unto us all things pertaining unto Life and Godliness. This leaves no room for us to boast in our "accomplishments or perfect observances." It leaves us boasting in the One made unto us all that He is. In view of this, Paul writes, *"That no flesh should glory in his presence. But of him are ye in Christ Jesus, who of God is made unto us wisdom, and righteousness, and*

---

[59] Ephesians 2:8-9

sanctification, and redemption: That, according as it is written, He that glorieth, let him glory in the Lord."[60] Christ is the Life and Righteousness the Law of Moses demanded but could not give. The grace of God is that He is that Life in us now.

Again, righteousness is a participation in and comprehension of the Life given of God. The Spirit works to bring us to such a participation and comprehension, which is fully captured in the statement, "Not I, but Christ liveth in me." I love that the commentary noted that righteousness achieved by man was never the expectation of the Law. It frustrates the natural mind to think that the Law, in which Paul found his boast at one time, never even expected man to arrive at the righteousness of which it spoke. That was never the intention. This is the struggle in Romans 7. Paul is not speaking of himself as one in Christ, but he is recalling the torment of the Law. I mentioned this already, but when Paul looked back at his time under the Law and was, in his pursuit of pleasing God, faced with the intent and expectation of the Law, he realized that he was not capable of meeting that expectation. It was not a matter of lack of zeal and effort, but it was a matter of nature, kind, and seed. The Law testified of another man. The Law leaned forward in expectation for the One who is of an altogether different nature and kind, the One who was not of corruptible seed. The righteousness of the Law has no natural fulfillment. It is only spiritually fulfilled, for it is fulfilled solely in the Spirit of Christ in us. In reference to this, Paul writes in Romans 7:14, *"For we know that the Law is Spiritual: but I am carnal, sold under sin."* Many people miss the true meaning of this verse. Paul, in looking back at his inward frustration as a zealous Jew, without the knowledge of God or the righteousness of God, sees that

---
[60] 1 Corinthians 1:29-31

the Law in its intention and expectation was spiritual. This means that the Law in its intent, in its expectation could only be spiritually fulfilled. I do not mean spiritual men fulfilling its intention, but the Spirit of Christ living in us as the fulfillment of its intention. How can we believe that man can fulfill the testimony, when Christ alone was the source of that testimony? The only thing the Law did to man was condemn him and his kind for not being the object that was in its view. It points the finger at the natural man and declares, "You are not HIM, and thereby you are condemned!" That is all the Law could do to man. It could not make him righteous in the sight of God. By the grace of God, we are partakers of HIM, who the Law cannot condemn.

That is why we are accepted IN (a union and relationship of rest) the Beloved.[61] Man, in his ignorance, assumed himself righteous by the Law. That happened, but the Law never expected it nor produced it, because it had a spiritual fulfillment in view. The Law always pointed to Christ, the Righteousness that would come and never to a righteousness that would be achieved. There is an eternal Truth upon which the entirety of the Law and prophets was based and that is Christ Himself. That is why we are faced with the intricacies of the testimony. That is why if anyone walked outside of the confines of that testimony they were killed or cast out of Israel. It was a perfect testimony with the perfect Truth as its basis. The things we in modern Christian religion attempt to establish as means of righteousness have absolutely no basis at all, but the observances of the Law had an eternal basis. Our salvation is not an extension of the external but spiritually expectant

---

[61] Ephesians 1:6
To the praise of the glory of His grace, in which He did make us accepted in the beloved. – Young's Literal Translation

testimony; salvation is the Spirit unto which the testimony pointed living in us.

Paul, understanding the union we now have with Christ, said it this way in Galatians 5:4, *"You have been severed from Christ, you who are seeking to be justified by Law; you have fallen from grace."*[62] He did not say you just made a mistake. He said you have fallen from grace. You have severed yourself from Christ. Paul is not condemning them to hell. This is not Paul questioning their salvation. He is saying you have forfeited the only relationship in which God relates to you. You have removed yourself from the realm of the satisfaction of the Father in order to try to satisfy Him on your own. What a perfect description of the inane pursuits of Christian religion today.

Grace has brought us into union with the Son of His own satisfaction, and if we are attempting to satisfy Him by any other means than the apprehension of that union, we have stepped outside of the confines of the fellowship He recognizes and in which He participates. In that state of heart, we are attempting to please God, as those alienated from the Son, of whom He said, "I am well pleased." We have walked outside of the predetermined boundaries of His satisfaction. The word "fallen" actually means to be outside of and thereby no longer experience a state or condition.[63] I stress again, that is exactly what the Spirit of God works toward in our hearts; to bring us to the experiential enjoyment of the salvation we have in Christ. If we seek something of reality outside of those eternally

---

[62] New American Standard - Updated

[63] NT:1601 ἐκπίπτω to no longer experience a state or condition - 'to be outside of, to experience no longer.' *(from Greek-English Lexicon Based on Semantic Domain. Copyright © 1988 United Bible Societies, New York. Used by permission.)*

determined perimeters, we impede the ability of the Spirit to work in us, for we are standing upon contrary ground. On that ground, we are not capable of experiencing Christ as God's satisfaction in us, but we are, in the darkness of our imagination, attempting to define His satisfaction by us.

We return to Paul saying, *"And be found in him, not having mine own righteousness, which is of the Law, but that which is through the faith of Christ, the righteousness which is of God by faith."* You can understand the power of that when you understand that the Law did not even expect man to become righteous by it. "Mine own" righteousness is not righteousness at all according to the intention of the Law. Paul is saying that righteousness is not that which is evidenced by external things, but is seen solely in the face of Jesus Christ. In other words, Paul was beholding the Truth; The Truth has appeared. The basis of the word "righteousness" has appeared and Paul was seen to be not it. Paul was seeing Him and for the excellency of the knowledge of Him, he suffered the loss of everything else. I do not think that Paul made these statements in the mindset we have imagined. Many imagine him mourning the loss of things that were gain to him. I believe he wrote the words joyously knowing that he had been released from an assumed righteousness, which kept him in bondage, and stood liberated to experience the Righteousness of God embodied in the indwelling Christ.

I have a diagram with which I will conclude this chapter. At the top of the diagram, we see all things in Christ before anything was made, before the foundation of the world. Paul says in Philippians 3:8, *"For whom I have suffered the loss of all things."* The phrase, "for whom" actually means by reason or in the light of whom I have suffered the loss. His thought is not that he has given up things of value for Jesus. The meaning is that in the light of eternal reality (the

Truth) he can now give up the illusion and false assumptions of possessing anything of his own through his works and observances. Light has to come first. You cannot give up an illusion when the Light has not appeared. All you will do then is create another illusion, maybe a more spiritual sounding illusion, but an illusion nonetheless. What does Paul mean by suffering the loss of all things? Notice this diagram again. Paul is saying, "All things defined by Me. righteousness, holiness, acceptance before the Father, relationship with God, perfection, etc. have been seen to be nothing at all in the revealed presence of the One who makes known, in His own Divine Being, the full exposition and measurement of those things."

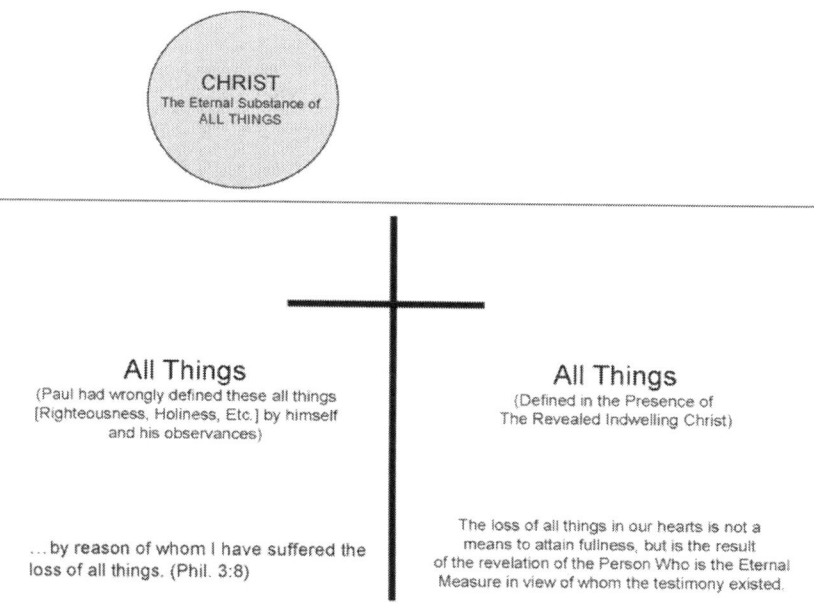

In Colossians 2:18, Paul speaks of those who are *"intruding into the things they have seen."* The Interlinear Bible and many other sources show that "not seen" is not the proper translation. "Not" is missing in the literal text of this verse.

They are intruding into things they have seen.[64] The things they have seen are the elements of the testimony; the elements of the Law. These "puffed up men" are looking at these now empty elements and because they are ignorant of the Person of their fulfillment, they have stepped into them and have become intruders. Intruding means to step your foot where it is not permitted.[65] They have stepped into those things and attempted to make themselves their measure and to become by religious observance the Truth of those things. What a perversion that is. When our concept of salvation and relationship with God goes no deeper than "seen things," we believe that we have to implement zealous adherence within the context of those "seen things" in order to satisfy God's heart. That is because we think God's perspective is also confined to those seen things, but God's perspective is and has always been the eternal Son that the natural eye can never see, but who must be revealed in us. The Father desires to unveil our souls to His own comprehension, so that our souls would be established within the eternal confines of our Great Salvation in the Person of the Son.

---

[64] Colossians 2:18
Paul, not stopping to discuss the nature of the things so seen, fixes on the radical error, the tendency of such a one to walk by SENSE (namely, what he haughtily prides himself on having SEEN), rather than by FAITH in the UNSEEN "Head" *(Jamieson, Fausset, and Brown Commentary, Electronic Database. Copyright © 1997, 2003, 2005, 2006 by Biblesoft, Inc. All rights reserved.)*

[65] NT:1687 embateuo (ἐμβατεύω, NT:1687), primarily, "to step in, or on" (from embaino, "to enter"), hence (a) "to frequent, dwell in," is used metaphorically in Colossians 2:18, RV, "dwelling in" (marg., "taking his stand upon") *(Vine's Expository Dictionary of Biblical Words, Copyright © 1985, Thomas Nelson Publishers.)*

NT:1687 ἐμβατεύω: The meaning of ἐμβατεύω, which occurs only once in the NT, namely, in Colossians 2:18, is obscure. It may mean more or less literally 'to set foot upon' or 'to enter' or possibly 'to come into possession of.' *(Greek-English Lexicon Based on Semantic Domain. Copyright © 1988 United Bible Societies, New York. Used by permission.)*

That is why God has given us His Spirit. The fact that the Truth of all things has come and that we are found in Him is the basis upon which the Spirit of God operates. 'Having begun in the Spirit..." The work of God in us is exclusively in accordance with where we begin. Because where we begin is where everything is found. Where we begin is also where God has His end. In the Son in whom we begin is the goal unto which all things pointed. The work of the Spirit is to bring the soul upon the proper ground of union with Christ, The Truth, who is the perfection of all things, in order that we may come to an inward participation in substance. Our souls are created for the real thing, which Real Thing abides in our hearts, and the work of the Spirit is toward our knowing and enjoyment of the Real. In the revealed presence of the Real (Eternal Substance / The Truth), the illusion and the misconception is joyously counted as nothing. In the clarity of His revealed presence, our hearts have one pursuit and that is to "apprehend that for which we have been apprehended of God". For any such apprehension to take place, we are absolutely dependant upon the Spirit of Truth to unveil our hearts to Christ in whom we live, move, and have our being.

God desires to establish our hearts within the confines of the union into which He has placed us. I have already shared Romans 2, where Paul writes, *"We have access by faith into the grace wherein we stand."* We stand in grace as those complete in Christ unto whom He is made all things of spiritual fullness and fulfillment. However, faith, which is the seeing of that "unseen evidence" accesses that grace. The Work of the Spirit is according to that grace to make known in our souls the full measure (the length, the depth, the breadth and the height) of the Son of God's eternal pleasure in whom we have begun.

CHAPTER THREE

...BUT WHEN IT PLEASED GOD

The New Covenant exists because our God is fully satisfied with His Finished Work. That Finished Work is embodied in His Son. The Old Covenant testified of God's intention and will. The New Covenant is the intention and will of the Father revealed and personified in the Son of His Love. That is why the New Covenant is not given on parchments and stones, but is written in our hearts.

In this chapter, I want to consider how God introduces the New Covenant and the effect of that introduction. We will do so by using the apostle Paul as an example. First, it is essential that we understand how dependent we are upon the Spirit of God to do what only He can do in our hearts. We will explore how God introduced the New Covenant historically, but we will also show how God does it in our hearts. There is no doubt that there were tremendous outward effects when God introduced the Person of the New Covenant, but that is but a speck when compared to the inward effects of such an introduction. If God does not introduce our salvation and the reality of the New Covenant in this specific way, we have no hope of comprehending or experiencing inwardly the New Covenant of which we have been made partakers by union with Christ. We can have the Life of God dwelling in us (and we do); we can have the fullness of Christ dwelling in us (and we do); but until our souls are introduced to Christ in whom all fullness dwells, we have no idea of the sufficiency and greatness of the salvation we have. That is the reason I believe most people are truly anticipating something more to come at a future date.

They have no comprehension of the **much more** and the surpassing excellence that has come in the Person of Christ.[66] God desires for our souls to observe Christ in such a way. T. Austin Sparks speaks of the *"all dominating and all governing vision of Christ"* that must be present in our souls. This God-given and soul-governing vision is essential to the believer's enjoyment of salvation, for it will keep our hearts from looking outside of Christ and seeking outside of our union with Him for anything of spiritual reality. That seems to be the unfortunate condition of the majority of Christians; they are attempting and expecting to perceive externally that which must be revealed and made known inwardly. The natural faculties do not possess the capacity to perceive eternal reality. The human body is not

---

[66] 2 Corinthians 3:9-11
For if the ministration of condemnation be glory, **much more** doth the ministration of righteousness exceed in glory. For even that which was made glorious had no glory in this respect, by reason of the glory that excelleth. For if that which is done away was glorious, **much more** that which remaineth is glorious.

Romans 5:17-20
For if by one man's offence death reigned by one; **much more** they which receive abundance of grace and of the gift of righteousness shall reign in life by one, Jesus Christ.) Therefore as by the offence of one judgment came upon all men to condemnation; even so by the righteousness of one the free gift came upon all men unto justification of life. For as by one man's disobedience many were made sinners, so by the obedience of one shall many be made righteous. Moreover the Law entered, that the offence might abound. But where sin abounded, grace did **much more** abound.

equipped with the proper instruments to behold such eternal fulfillment, but the soul was furnished with the faculties specifically designed to behold that which is above (in heavenly places in Christ). However, even those faculties, such as the eyes of the soul, must be *"flooded with the light of the knowledge of the glory of God in the face of Jesus Christ"*[67] to know that for which it was created. JP Phillips calls it the "inner illumination brought about by the Spirit."

That is beautifully depicted by John in the twenty-first chapter of the Revelation of Jesus Christ. John writes, *"And the city has no need of the sun nor of the moon to illuminate it, for the glory of God illuminated it, and its lamp is the Lamb."*[68] What makes this so tremendous is the fact that the word translated as enlightened or illuminated spoken of in Ephesians 1 is the same Greek word that is used in Revelation 21. Notice the condition of that city in such a state of enlightenment, for it speaks of the condition of our souls when they are filled with the Light of Christ's revealed presence. It states that the city had *"**no need** of sun or moon to illuminate it."* It had no need of "natural light." The indwelling presence of Christ and the glory of God and the Lamb did illuminate it. When our hearts are being enlightened in the coming of the indwelling Christ, we have no need for the vain imaginations, concepts, and insights of the natural mind.

---

[67] Ephesians 1:17-18
That the God of our Lord Jesus Christ, the Father of glory, may give to you a Spirit of wisdom and revelation in *the* full knowledge of Him, the eyes of your mind having been enlightened, for you to know what is the hope of His calling, and what *are* the riches of the glory of His inheritance in the saints. – J.P. Greene LitV

[68] Revelations 21:13 from The New Testament: An Expanded Translation by Kenneth S. Wuest *(Copyright © 1961 by Wm. B. Eerdmans Publishing Co. All rights reserved.)*

A few years ago, a precious brother in Christ came and spoke to me about a sense of separation from God that he was experiencing. He told me that it seemed the more he sought to be close to God and desired to know God, he sensed a greater feeling of distance from God than ever before. It was not difficult for me to relate to his situation at all because I had also encountered a very similar time in my own Christian experience. It was during that time that God took me to the Tabernacle and specifically the Holiest of All. There is something very specific with regard to this room that must be understood in the context of our salvation. Remember, if we are in Christ, we are in the Holiest of All, but here is the strange and wonderful truth concerning this place. The construct of that room made it entirely impossible for any shred of natural light to penetrate that foursquare space. This made it impossible for anything to be known in that place save the Glory of God appears. I told that brother that he was not actually experiencing distance from God; it was his concept of what it meant to be close to God that was being taken away. His natural "light" is not permitted within the confines of Christ. The same is true with us. To know the Truth of our salvation, which is not clouded by our precious illusions, the Lord of Glory must appear and be the Light in which we walk and by which we see. When that is the state of our soul, there is no need of natural light, for God hath shined in our hearts.

John writes, *"As for you, the anointing which you received from Him abides in you, and you have no need for anyone to teach you; but as His anointing teaches you about all things, and is true and is not a lie, and just as it has taught you, you abide in Him."*[69] This in no way diminishes the need for teachers of the gospel; it does not even imply that

---

[69] 1 John 2:27 – New American Standard

there is no need for teachers of the gospel. The meaning is that "with regard to the learning and knowing of the Truth," man is not your source. We, as ministers, speak in accordance to the Truth we are beholding Christ to be in us. However, for the hearer or reader actually to experience the reality of that gospel, they must turn and submit their own souls, so that the Spirit may do in them what is not in the capacity of any man to do. We have to understand that the knowing of Christ is not from without, but from within. I do not mean that we do not preach and teach the word, but I cannot nor can any other man teach you the reality that God has established in His Son, only the Spirit can teach you this established fact of God and He does it by revealing that Son in us.

Paul was a man schooled from his earliest days in the Torah. He was taught the letter of the scripture all of his life and, based upon that teaching, he performed and observed all the things that he assumed would cause him to live acceptably before God. Paul had a heart to serve God and walk uprightly before Him. He found his life and his boasting in his unblemished adherence to the Law's demands. This is the great gain of which he speaks. There is much we could say about this, but I want to just share with you something I feel makes the point very succinctly. First, we must look at Philippians 3:7-9, *"But what things were gain to me, those I counted loss for Christ. Yea doubtless, and I count all things but loss for the excellency of the knowledge of Christ Jesus my Lord: for whom I have suffered the loss of all things, and do count them but dung, that I may win Christ, And be found in him, not having mine own righteousness, which is of the Law, but that which is through the faith of Christ, the righteousness which is of God by faith."* John Calvin says the following in his commentary of these verses. *"Paul renounced everything that he had, that he might recover them in Christ; and this corresponds better with the word gain, for it means that it was no trivial or ordinary gain, inasmuch as Christ contains everything in himself. And, unquestionably, we lose nothing when we come to Christ naked and stript. Of everything, for those things, which we previously imagined, on false grounds, that we possessed, we then begin really to acquire. He, accordingly, shews more fully, how great the riches of Christ, because we obtain and find all things in him."* When Paul says that he counted all things that were gain to him as loss or as dung, we must understand that to Paul it was not deemed a great loss in the light of the exceeding glory of the revealed Christ. He merely reckoned as dung what was already reckoned of God to be dung. The righteousness that he supposed himself to possess as a zealous Jew was seen to be nothing but filthy rags in the appearing of the Righteousness of God. In the light of the knowledge of the Glory of God in the face of Jesus Christ, Paul realized that none of the things that he held to and deemed spiritually profitable, were of any value at all. In fact, his reference to dung takes us back to the Old Covenant and the necessity to remove the dung outside of the camp of Israel and burn it outside of the camp. This relates to what is of man, what is of flesh. In the light of the revealed Christ, Paul is actually saying, "all that I am, everything that I vainly perceived to be defined and measured by myself and my activities are nothing but the dung of a dead sacrifice and it is worthless and to hold to it would actually bring contamination to the heart."

Paul counts it ALL as loss and he does not attempt to keep what he considers "the best of the herd" or the "good parts" of those external activities which accomplished nothing but "self righteousness and deception." Paul was beholding reality in the appearing of Christ and all else was seen to be falsehood and refuse. Again, for Paul, righteousness came to be defined in the face of the Truth. Now, Christ has appeared as the Righteousness of God, which Paul had imagined upon false ground that he possessed before seeing Christ. Paul came face to face with the consummation and eternal realization of every expectation he possessed as a zealous adherent to the Jewish religion. What a wonderful thing it would be if every born again Christian would come to such an encounter. They would cease to live with vain expectations and actually behold the One Yea and Amen of the divine expectation. For this is that for which we are created, we are born again for that face to face relationship and participation with Christ.

It is impossible to participate in the reality into which you have been brought until you see Him as present. There is no way, for until we see Him, our souls will be convinced that what we have is real or we will be waiting on a human invented "reality" to come. The Alexandrian Church Father Athanasius[70] wrote of those under the Old Covenant as being *"exercised in the types as a preparation for the Reality."* That is how he worded it, and that is a great way to say it. However, the sad part is the majority of Christians still live in that manner. We do not live under the valid types and figures; we have merely invented more things that are external. Religion promises that they prepare us for reality, but they only keep us blind to the reality that is present in Christ. Most have been programmed to think that God is preparing us for reality; the truth is He has brought us to the only reality there is! As we wrote in the previous chapter, the Spirit of God works exclusively upon that basis. The Spirit of God does not work upon anything short of or any premise less than reality, perfection, and fullness

---

[70] On the incarnation: the treatise De incarnatione Verbi Dei; A.R. Mowbray - 1953

in Christ. He never has and He never will. We who are in Christ must allow the Spirit of Truth to awaken our hearts to who is present. For the Spirit of Truth to work upon any basis less than Truth would be for Him to work in our hearts contrary to His own Finished Work. He does not do that.

God works in us to awaken our souls to the One who is His pleasure. We have already read it in Matthew 3:14-17, *"But John forbad him, saying, I have need to be baptized of thee, and comest thou to me? And Jesus answering said unto him, Suffer it to be so now: for thus it becometh us to fulfil all righteousness. Then he suffered him. And Jesus, when he was baptized, went up straightway out of the water: and, lo, the heavens were opened unto him, and he saw the Spirit of God descending like a dove, and lighting upon him: And lo a voice from heaven, saying, This is my beloved Son, in whom I am well pleased."* As I have pointed out, the J.P. Greene Literal Version reads, *"This is My Son in whom I have been delighting."* In the Greek, it is in the aorist tense, which means that it speaks of something that has past occurrence with active present effect. It is not something that happened at that moment, but God declaring at that moment what is eternally true. There has never been a moment when He has not been God's pleasure. Proverbs 8 tells us that. He always stood before His Father as His delight, as His pleasure. Now He is present and God introduces this One as the Beginning and the Ending, as the Substance of the New Covenant. This is how God introduced the New Covenant. THIS is the One in whom I am well pleased. Everything else spoke of, testified of, and even pointed toward God's pleasure saying in unison: "He is coming." Paul writes about the good thing that was to come; the good thing that the types, shadows and elements of the Old Covenant presented as yet to come. However, He does not leave it as an unfulfilled promise; Paul declares "the good thing is now IN YOU." That is what I am presenting in this book. This is My Beloved Son, the good thing promised. Again, we looked at Genesis 1 when God observed the things He had done, He saw that it was very good, and He rested from His works. It is the same here, "This is very good. This is where I find my pleasure. This is my Sabbath. He is the end of my work."

This Son was the Eternal basis for everything God did. Paul says it very plainly: *"For by Him all things were made that are made. By Him all things are created."* Why? HE was the Father's perspective. He was the object in view and I am not only looking at the natural creation. I am talking about the testimony of it. We see in Matthew 17, God presenting this Son as the delight of whom Moses (Law) and Elijah (Prophets) were capable merely to testify. God is saying in that moment, they are they, which testified of this Beloved Son, now He has come as their summation – Hear Him. Peter speaks of our having "a more sure word of prophesy." He looks back at this very instance for the basis of that statement. It was an external picture of an inward work of God, wherein He reveals this Son as the end of the testimony, the amen to the promises, and the substance of every expectation. Futurism teachers still would have us believe that such is not the case at all.

The problem can be condensed down to the fact that we are attempting to perceive that which is Spirit through the weakness of human perception and intellect. That into which we have come is something that can only be seen by FAITH; meaning it can only be revealed by God. You cannot observe it externally. Jesus said two statements that seem so contradictory. In John 3:3, He says, *"Verily, verily, I say unto thee, Except a man be born again, he cannot see the kingdom of God."* Then in Luke 17:20, He says, *"The kingdom of God cometh not with observation."* Now how can you see a Kingdom that cannot be seen? The fact is that Jesus is speaking here of another type of sight that is involved when it pertains to the Kingdom of God. The word for "observation" there is ocular evidence.[71] The evidence of the Kingdom cannot be seen with the natural eye. That is true with everything spiritual; that is true with everything real because what is spiritual is what is real. What is spiritual is what is literal. When we think literal, we wrongly think of what we can touch. The literal thing is what Spirit is because there is a spiritual basis for everything else. That is literal. So when they say do you believe in a "literal coming" of Christ? I answer yes I do; I believe in a very literal coming of Christ that takes place in my soul. That is literal because in Christ, we have come from the natural to the spiritual. 1 Corinthians 15:46, *"Howbeit that was not first which is Spiritual, but that which is natural; and afterward that which is Spiritual."* Every time the word "afterward" is used in the scripture, it is speaking about the New Covenant; it is always speaking of that which is Spirit.

We have come to the spiritual fullness of every naturally observable type. However, that is only observed, only perceived when faith comes; when God makes it known in the face of His Son. That is why Jesus can say in Matthew

---

[71] NT:3907 παρατήρησις parateresis (par-at-ay'-ray-sis); from NT:3906; inspection, i.e. ocular evidence: KJV – observation. *(Biblesoft's New Exhaustive Strong's Numbers and Concordance with Expanded Greek-Hebrew Dictionary. Copyright © 1994, 2003, 2006 Biblesoft, Inc. and International Bible Translators, Inc.)*

parateresis (παρατήρησις, NT:3907), "attentive watching" (akin to paratereo, "to observe"), is used in Luke 17:20, of the manner in which the kingdom of God (i. e., the operation of the Spiritual kingdom in the hearts of men) does not come, "in such a manner that it can be watched with the eyes" (Grimm-Thayer), or, as KJV marg., "with outward show." *(Vine's Expository Dictionary of Biblical Words, Copyright © 1985, Thomas Nelson Publishers.)*

17:20, *"I say unto you, if ye have faith as a grain of mustard seed, ye shall say unto this mountain, Remove hence to yonder place; and it shall remove..."* To what mountain is He referring? He is speaking of Sinai, the mountain that stood in opposition to Zion, the one that stood in opposition to the coming of the newness of the New Covenant itself. You can say to this mountain be thou removed and be cast into the yonder places because the revealing of the spiritual fulfillment dispels the need for external evidences and constrains the gaze of the soul within the boundaries of Christ alone. This is what happens when God introduces the New Covenant as only He can. This is My Beloved Son. This is He, hear Him, behold Him. This is the One who I have always beheld, and now He is here for YOU to see. The Spirit of God is not going to work upon anything less than that. He is never going to work upon anything less than the presence of Christ in the soul, and the soul's desperate need of seeing Him and growing in the knowledge of Him.

We attempt to perceive righteousness by looking at men, their activities, their actions, and the things in which they involve themselves. We attempt to perceive holiness by what people wear or what they do not wear. The seeing of Christ, however, affects an inward separation from such external things. That separation never ceases for a heart that is turned to see Him, because that moment of seeing Him never ends. It is a perpetual moment. In this ongoing appearing of Christ, there is always a severing from what we have assumed to be valid and of spiritual benefit.

We see this in the life of Paul. Paul writes in Galatians 1:15-16, *"But when it pleased God, who separated me from my mother's womb, and called me by his grace, To reveal his Son in me, that I might preach him among the heathen; immediately I conferred not with flesh and blood."* He speaks here of being SEPARATED from his mother's womb. Many who read this phrase will inevitably interpret it as meaning Paul's natural birth from the womb of his natural mother. I do not totally dismiss that this verse could be used to present the fact that Paul understood that the revealing of Christ was the only reason for him ever to be born of a woman. However, the aforementioned interpretation does not fit with the context of the letter. It is my conviction that he is speaking of the womb of Old Covenant Judaism, the religion of the Jews. This corresponds to the "mother" he writes of in Galatians 4 who is in bondage with her children: the mother whose children are not heirs, because the heir is the SEED Himself. Now, consider the tremendous work of God that could bring about such an awesome transition in the heart of this man.

This is why the term separated is very important to the meaning of this verse and the letter as a whole. Paul is previously describing his manner of life under the Law and all that he accomplished as a zealous Pharisee, but now he is showing how God transformed him from the zealous adherent to the Law and persecutor of the church to the prisoner of Jesus Christ and the one proclaiming Him as the end of the Law. The term as it is actually defined gives us a true glimpse of the effects that this revelation of Christ wrought in the heart of Paul and will bring about in ours as well.

In the Greek the word separated is aphorizo ἀφορίζω which means *to set off by boundary, i.e. (figuratively) limit, exclude, divide, separate, sever.*[72] This shows us that this

---

[72] NT:873 ἀφορίζω aphorizo (af-or-id'-zo); from NT:575 and NT:3724; to set off by boundary, i.e. (figuratively) limit, exclude, appoint, etc. KJV - divide, separate, sever. *(Biblesoft's New Exhaustive Strong's Numbers and Concordance with Expanded Greek-Hebrew Dictionary. Copyright © 1994, 2003, 2006 Biblesoft, Inc. and International Bible Translators, Inc.)*

separation is not primarily from something, but is into the boundaries of a sphere or place. When God revealed Christ in Paul's soul, the eternal dimensions of salvation were, for the first time, clearly defined and the walls of salvation were erected, thus severing his soul from all that had no place within those borders.

This is beautifully depicted in Nehemiah when the city is restored; the walls of the city are fully built, or in other words the work is finished. We then read in Nehemiah 8:1-8, *"And all the people gathered themselves together as one man into the street that was before the water gate; and they spake unto Ezra the scribe to bring the book of the Law of Moses, which the Lord had commanded to Israel. And Ezra the priest brought the Law before the congregation both of men and women, and all that could hear with understanding, upon the first day of the seventh month. And he read therein before the street that was before the water gate from the morning until midday, before the men and the women, and those that could understand; and the ears of all the people were attentive unto the book of the Law. And Ezra the scribe stood upon a pulpit of wood, which they had made for the purpose; and beside him stood Mattithiah, and Shema, and Anaiah, and Urijah, and Hilkiah, and Maaseiah, on his right hand; and on his left hand, Pedaiah, and Mishael, and Malchiah, and Hashum, and Hashbadana, Zechariah, and Meshullam. And Ezra opened the book in the sight of all the people; (for he was above all the people;) and when he opened it, all the people stood up: And Ezra blessed the Lord, the great God. And all the people answered, Amen, Amen, with lifting up their hands: and they bowed their heads, and worshipped the Lord with their faces to the ground. Also Jeshua, and Bani, and Sherebiah, Jamin, Akkub, Shabbethai, Hodijah, Maaseiah, Kelita, Azariah, Jozabad, Hanan, Pelaiah, and the Levites, caused the people to understand the Law: and the people stood in their place. So they read in the book in the Law of God distinctly,* **and gave the sense, and caused them to understand the reading.**" Notice, they did not just read the Law of God, but the sense and the understanding of the Law was given. This has a tremendous effect. There is always an effect, not from merely reading the words, but beholding the meaning of the words in the presence of Christ. Even the phrase "caused them to understand" has the meaning "to give an understanding that brings about a mental separation."[73] In this revealing of Christ, Paul, who was under the Law all of His life, finally came face to face with the sense (intention) and meaning of the Law of God. For Paul and for us, the separation is far greater and runs far deeper than mental. Therefore, as we proceed in this narrative, we see the outworking of that understanding. Nehemiah 9:2, *"And the seed of Israel separated themselves from all strangers."* In the Hebrew, the word "strangers" actually speaks of the strange seed, the sons that were produced in mixture. Paul faced this same separation in his own heart. The Seed of God, The Israel of God has appeared and now his soul is severed from any relationship with the false seed (natural Israel, Adam). Therefore, he can say that the inheritance does not belong to the multitude of natural seeds, but the One Seed unto whom all the promises were made. Until that Seed appears within, we will always attempt to lay claim to the inheritance that belongs solely to Him. Nehemiah 10:28, *"And the rest of the people, the priests, the Levites, the porters, the singers, the Nethinims, and all they that had separated themselves from the people of the lands unto the Law of God, their wives, their sons, and their daughters, every one having knowledge, and having understanding."* Notice again, this separation is

---

[73] OT:995 בִּין biyn (bene); a primitive root; to separate mentally (or distinguish), i.e.(generally) understand. *(Biblesoft's New Exhaustive Strong's Numbers and Concordance with Expanded Greek-Hebrew Dictionary. Copyright © 1994, 2003, 2006 Biblesoft, Inc. and International Bible Translators, Inc.)*

from the people of strange lands due to it being UNTO THE LAW OF GOD (revealed and understood). It goes on to read that these who separated themselves were those who had knowledge and understanding. This separation is always predicated upon the coming of knowledge and understanding. Nehemiah 13:3, *"Now it came to pass, when they had heard the Law, that they separated from Israel all the mixed multitude."* We see that after this separation was complete, only The Pure Seed remained. This takes place in the heart of the believer who beholds the Son of God. He is seen to be the only One that remains. This is the effect. The revealing of Christ clearly sets before us the landscape of a vast reality that He will make known as we set our hearts to know; while also unrelentingly excluding all else; previous concepts, ideologies and doctrinal agreement; all that had self as its measure and meaning.

This takes us back to Paul. The separation of which he is speaking is two fold. It is both objective and subjective. The grace of God has brought him into Christ and he has by reason of that work been translated from darkness to Light, death to Life. However, this inward unveiling of the soul brought him to an inward acknowledgement and enjoyment of that grace. The seeing of Christ unveils our souls unto the predestined boundaries of the New Covenant and defines the place in which we will and must discover all fullness; do not allow the vain philosophies of men to cause you to look elsewhere and be deceived. That is the wonderful side effect of this separation. It constrains the soul within the realm of eternal perfection and therefore guards the soul from deception.

It is in such a state that Paul can now look at all else, even those things he says were gain to him, and understand that they are of no value at all. You cannot do that until there has been a severing. You will try to hold on to as much of it as you can, assuming it to be of God. I am realizing on a daily basis, in the seeing of Christ, that all I have assumed as valid and good in my own mind has always been dung! This has to take place or we will always substitute the external for the eternal and totally disregard all that has been given to us in Christ. The inward sight becomes the overriding sight needing no external supplementation. That is the understanding to which the Spirit of God would bring us so that we no longer look and seek reality in the things that are seen. Please understand that I am not talking about your car and your television, I am speaking of the externally observable things that we have misconstrued and misinterpreted as spiritually relevant.

God introduced Paul's soul to the reality He had awaited all of his life and in that Light he was able to relinquish his grasp on everything he at one time deemed to be gain. It is impossible to release our grip on what we still deem as spiritually valid and beneficial until the reality of heaven arises in our hearts. If this does not take place and we do not turn and submit our hearts to this work of God, we will still call our darkness light and our ignorance knowledge. We must understand that the things Paul were counting as dung at one time had spiritual credence. This is a testament to the power of this work known as the revelation of Jesus Christ.

It is in this state of separation that Paul writes a stern warning to the Philippians. In Philippians 3, Paul gives a little more detailed account of his life as a zealous Jew than the one we read in Galatians 1:13-14. As I studied it, I was struck by something that never had occurred to me before and it has to do with a warning he gives to this church. Such a warning could never come from a heart that has not faced the severing work of the appearing of Christ. In Philippians 3:2, we read, *"Beware of dogs, beware of evil* *workers, beware of **the concision.**"* He is writing about Jews, specifically zealous Jews, as he was, who would attempt to seduce them toward the bondage of the Law. The thing that truly intrigued me in this verse was Paul's description of these religiously motivated Jews, again as he previously was. He calls them the concision and warns the Philippians to beware of them. To expose my ignorance, I will admit that I always assumed that the word merely meant natural circumcision. However, Paul uses the term concision for a very specific reason. What does concision mean? Keep in mind we are speaking of a man that has experienced an inward transition and severing from the natural and external elements of the testimony, to the spiritual and inward substance of the testimony. This word perfectly demonstrates the depth of that transition. The word concision is defined as ***the mutilators***.[74] Commentaries agree that Paul is using a paronomasia or wordplay, but this is not a lighthearted turn of phrase; this is a stern warning that is based upon a spiritual comprehension and judgment that Paul is personally experiencing. What a tremendous change for this man who was a circumcised Jew himself to now be able to say that those who would give validity to an external cutting away of flesh are nothing more than mutilators. What took place? What happened? Did they change the kind of blade they

---

[74] NT:2699 κατατομή katatome (kat-at-om-ay'); from a compound of NT:2596 and temno (to cut); a cutting down (off), i.e. mutilation (ironically): KJV - concision. *(Biblesoft's New Exhaustive Strong's Numbers and Concordance with Expanded Greek-Hebrew Dictionary. Copyright © 1994, 2003, 2006 Biblesoft, Inc. and International Bible Translators, Inc.)*

katatome (κατατομή, NT:2699), lit., "a cutting off" (kata, "down," temno, "to cut"), "a mutilation," is a term found in Philippians 3:2, there used by the apostle, by a paronomasia, contemptuously, for the Jewish circumcision with its Judaistic influence, in contrast to the true Spiritual circumcision. *(Vine's Expository Dictionary of Biblical Words, Copyright © 1985, Thomas Nelson Publishers.)*

used to cut? Did they change the technique of circumcision? It should be obvious that it was a much deeper matter for Paul. The transition from a man who gloried in his external circumcision to a man that called it mutilation of the body was the result of beholding the spiritual embodiment and reality unto which those external elements pointed. The point is that the change was not external but internal. Attempting to relate to God by those external things instead of through an inward acknowledgement of the sufficiency of the indwelling Christ was seen by Paul to be the greatest perversion. When the eternal boundaries of salvation are defined in our hearts, there is found no room for anything but the knowing and Spirit-guided discovery of the dimensions of the glorious Christ of God. The beholding of the excellency of the Son of God had severed Paul's soul from all that had previously defined reality in his heart, whether it be birthright, lineage, religious education, etc. Paul desired such a severance to be experienced in the soul of every born again person, so that they may apprehend the fullness into which they have been apprehended of God. Therefore, he warns them against anyone who would attempt to bring validity to any of those things and cause them to miss the reality that is exclusively found in the face of Christ Himself.

The thing we must keep in mind is that these mutilators, those he called the concision, were just like Paul was at one time, and they were with all of their hearts, sold out to the fact that they were pleasing God. They thought they were. We read where Paul says in Acts 26:9, *"I verily thought with myself, that I ought to do many things contrary to the name of Jesus of Nazareth."* He was totally convinced that in all of the things he did, he pleased God. He tells the Jews and their leaders in Acts 22:1-21, speaking to them in the Hebrew tongue. He spoke to them of being taught by Gamaliel to the perfect letter of the Law, proclaiming himself as being zealous toward God just as they were. He speaks of all of the things that he did, supposing them to be pleasing to God, but what is it that brought his heart from that false supposition to truly comprehending the pleasure of God? HE SAW THE LORD. He came to a face to face, soul transforming and transitioning encounter with the risen Christ, the long awaited Messiah. Such an encounter was the basis and the catalyst for this great division that took place in his soul. Paul did not encounter another circumcision that made a cut and left a scar, but he experienced a heart circumcision that cut off an entire creation and man and left nothing but Christ.

This seems simple but this is the necessity for the soul. The soul was actually created to be introduced to the present Christ as the embodiment of the New Covenant. Notice that the New Covenant is introduced in this way. My pleasure is perfectly fulfilled in this My Beloved Son. After such an introduction, what else is there except HIM? What else is there? The boundaries of God's delight were revealed. Hear HIM. Everything the Law and Prophets declared, pointed to this moment. Now if we are to hear God, we will hear Him in His Son. The Son is the Father's eternal summary statement. God has nothing more to say. He has sent His Word. Christ is The Word that went forth out of the Father and accomplished His pleasure. The Son has not returned unto His Father void.

Christ has fulfilled God's pleasure and He **is** God's pleasure.[75] He is that pleasure in you and in me! Please understand that it is not only in these accounts that God

---

[75] Isaiah 55:11
So is My word that goeth out of My mouth, It turneth not back unto Me empty, But hath done that which I desired, And prosperously effected that [for] which I sent it. – Young's Literal Translation

desires to introduce the New Covenant; it is in you and it is in me. The fact is that you can have the full reality of the New Covenant dwelling in your heart and still have no idea of the New Covenant, and still not enjoy the reality of the New Covenant and be living as if you are not there. That is why most are still living as if they are still waiting for something more. However, the New Covenant exists because God is fully satisfied. It could not exist if God was not completely satisfied. The love of God toward us is that He has chosen to share that satisfaction with the soul. What a tragedy that most Christians are refusing such a glorious gift.

The New Covenant does not exist for a future consummation: the New Covenant exists AS the consummation of God. The consummation Himself, the Beginning and the End, is the New Covenant. God introduces that Covenant by revealing The Son in the soul. He did it historically but He now desires to do the same inwardly. There is nothing more beyond Him. It is the lack or the absence of seeing Christ that has caused the misguided teachings of futurism that would have us believe that God Himself is as unsatisfied as we are. In the opinion of futurists, we cannot be satisfied with our salvation because God is not yet satisfied. God is just as unsatisfied as we are. One day He will be satisfied and we can be too. That is what they would tell us, but that is because their hearts have not come to God's point of view, God's perspective, God's understanding. God's perspective is not me and God's view is not you. He does not look at man to define His satisfaction. He never has. He does not look at events to fulfill His satisfaction. He never has and He never will. I do not care how many events we may imagine – He does not. His satisfaction is set. It is done whether you can see it or not. That is why it is Truth: whether you see it, like it, accept it or not – it is TRUTH. It is The Truth. God's work is to attempt to bring your soul to the acknowledgment of The Truth. That was Paul's heart in 2 Timothy 2:10, *"For this reason I endure all things for the sake of those who are chosen, so that they also may obtain the salvation which is in Christ Jesus and with it eternal glory."*[76] The word "attain" there does not mean to get something you do not have: it means to enjoy and experience something that is present.

We think God is dependent as we are on the seeing of outward things. But God's satisfaction is fixed and settled. It is not a work in progress, but the eternal basis upon which God has always worked. He does not work toward a goal, but He has always worked in view of the Goal who stands before Him. God does not work as we do. Isaiah 46:10, *"Declaring the end from the beginning, and from ancient times the things that are not yet done, saying, My counsel shall stand, and I will do all my pleasure."* He does not work toward an end, He works in view of The End. He works in view of the One who pleases Him eternally, and He works in us according to that same view. The need of our soul and the purpose of the Spirit's work in us is that we come to behold and comprehend The One who is the fixed and settled pleasure of God.

This brings me to the point I want to make in this chapter. Galatians 1:13-16, *"For ye have heard of my conversation in time past in the Jews' religion, how that beyond measure I persecuted the church of God, and wasted it: And profited in the Jews' religion above many my equals in mine own nation, being more exceedingly zealous of the traditions of my fathers."* (These words "profited" and "gain to me" in Philippians 3 are conveying the same thought, even though they are not the same Greek words). *But when it pleased*

---

[76] New American Standard Updated

God, who separated me from my mother's womb, and called me by his grace, To reveal his Son in me, that I might preach him among the heathen; immediately I conferred not with flesh and blood." I want to emphasize this small portion: BUT WHEN IT **PLEASED GOD** TO REVEAL HIS SON IN ME. I want us to see something I think is significant. I do not want to upset anyone's theology, but I have been looking at this a little differently. It is the pleasure of the Father to reveal His Son. I will never discount that; it is true.

But the question that came into my heart a few weeks ago was – why? We can make the blanket statement and say it is God's pleasure to reveal His Son in you, but the question comes to me, Why is it His pleasure to reveal His Son? The answer is in view of the words I have stressed in this book – Satisfaction and Pleasure. I believe it to be significant that Paul used the term pleased in this verse. He did not just say, after all of that time under the Law, God revealed His Son in me. I do not believe that Paul ever used vain words and here his words are significant and deliberate. BUT when it PLEASED God. He writes the same thing in Philippians 3:7, *"But what things were gain to me, those I counted loss for Christ."* The word "but" in Galatians 1, according to Thayer's Lexicon is *"a word that is used as a marker of contrast, and it serves to mark a transition into something altogether new."* That is why it is so significant here that Paul first talks about his time under the Law and gives what could be looked at as a very impressive resume that would present him to be a very impressive man under the Law. He was a man who boasted in his Law keeping, as a Pharisee of Pharisees.

It is also interesting that the word "Pharisee" means separated.[77] So when Paul says in these verses that God separated him, there is a much greater meaning presented. The fact is that when he was a Pharisee, Paul's measure of being separated was within the context of circumcised or uncircumcised, clean or unclean. This concept of separation was measured by natural standards, by external religious observations. The Jews were clean and holy, the Gentiles were unclean, and sinners, all of these distinctions were based upon outward measures. However, in the light of the inward appearing of Christ, Paul was facing a separation that was so much deeper than nationalities, religious ceremonies, and observances. He is no longer separated by dogma and doctrine. There is an inward work of the Spirit of Truth separating him from earth to heaven, from darkness to light, from illusions to reality, from types to Truth, and from promises to Person.

Patriarchal traditions and Laws no longer separate him from others. Now his soul has seen the only thing that remains in the sight of God and his soul has been separated unto the Father's exclusive and eternal view. This corresponds with Paul's statement in Romans 1:1, *"Paul, a servant of Jesus Christ, called to be an apostle, separated unto the gospel of God."* Again, this is reflected in the transfiguration. It reads

---

[77] NT:5330 pharisaios (φαρισαῖος, NT:5330), from an Aramaic word peras (found in Daniel 5:28), signifying "to separate," owing to a different manner of life from that of the general public. *(Vine's Expository Dictionary of Biblical Words, Copyright © 1985, Thomas Nelson Publishers.)*

NT:5330
Apparently the Pharisees were concerned above all with the sanctification of God's name (cf. Ap. ii.171, 192) and with the separation from all that was unholy. Their name also alludes to this emphasis (Φαρισαῖοι and π'ρûZΓμ refer to "separated ones"), which their adversaries used in the derogatory sense of "separatists."*(Exegetical Dictionary of the New Testament © 1990 by William B. Eerdmans Publishing Company. All rights reserved.)*

that they lifted up their eyes and saw no man, save Jesus only. The word ONLY there means only or alone; it also means what is remaining.[78] One word study says that it speaks to the exclusivity of a thing or a person. We are dealing with the exclusive view of the New Covenant. God introduces the New Covenant by introducing and making known the exclusivity of His view by revealing His Son. Paul refers to the very same thing by saying in 2 Corinthians 11:3, *"But I fear, lest by any means, as the serpent beguiled Eve through his subtilty, so your minds should be corrupted from the simplicity that is in Christ."* The word "simplicity" means singleness and it speaks to the exclusiveness of Christ and the singleness of the Father's perspective. We must realize in our souls that the only thing that remains in the Father's line of sight is the One who has eternally occupied that place: Christ. This is presented to us several times in the testimony of scripture. Genesis 7:23, *"And every living substance was destroyed which was upon the face of the ground, both man, and cattle, and the creeping things, and the fowl of the heaven; and they were destroyed from the earth: and Noah only remained alive, and they that were with him in the ark."* What a definition of the New Creation. There are not multitudes of people that remain alive after the judgment of the Cross (the true flood), there is but One who remains alive and lives as the Life of all who would live in newness of Life. Therefore, He lives and He is the Life of all who are found to be with or in union with Him. The singleness and exclusivity of God's view is presented here.

---

[78] NT:3440 μόνον monon (mon'-on); neuter of NT:3441 as adverb; merely: KJV - alone, but, only.

NT:3441 μόνος monos (mon'-os); probably from NT:3306; remaining, i.e. sole or single; by implication mere: KJV - alone, only, by themselves.
(Biblesoft's New Exhaustive Strong's Numbers and Concordance with Expanded Greek-Hebrew Dictionary. Copyright © 1994, 2003, 2006 Biblesoft, Inc. and International Bible Translators, Inc.)

1 Samuel 16:10-12, *"Again, Jesse made seven of his sons to pass before Samuel. And Samuel said unto Jesse, The Lord hath not chosen these. And Samuel said unto Jesse, Are here all thy children? And he said, There remaineth yet the youngest, and, behold, he keepeth the sheep. And Samuel said unto Jesse, Send and fetch him: for we will not sit down till he come hither. And he sent, and brought him in. Now he was ruddy, and withal of a beautiful countenance, and goodly to look to. And the Lord said, Arise, anoint him: for this is he."* After God's rejection of those who would "seem" to be acceptable according to the natural eye, there is a question posed? Is this all of them? This question resonates in my heart because it is the exact question that I posed to God many years ago. I was aware that God had rejected everything I had presented to Him, so I cried out, "God, is there not more, is this everything; there has to be more than this?" Oh, then came the answer. There remains One. Then God brought my soul face to face with Him and declared within me with resounding force – Arise, for this is He. Here is the King I have chosen. Has God said that in you? You must experience this declaration in your heart. The glorious good news of the Grace of God is that there remains One and He is in you now. Set your heart's affection to see Him, for it is the Father's pleasure to make Him known. Unfortunately, our soul's attention can easily be swayed from that single object of God's own pleasure if we are not perpetually living in His appearing. We will easily be caught up and distracted with what we believe remains and what we suppose has validity in the sight of God. This is why it is the pleasure of the Father to reveal His Son, because it is in that moment (perpetual moment) that the soul He created is awakened to His exclusive and singular view. In that moment the Father is able to share His eternal pleasure with the soul He has created. The necessity for us is the exclusive view of the Father being revealed in us. This revelation was not merely necessary

historically; the necessity for His inward revealing is much more upon us because the soul must be introduced to the New Covenant to discern anything of it and to experience anything of the salvation that is present. If this is not taking place in us, friends, we will still live as if we are waiting for some assumed divine loose ends to be tied together. What a terrible state of darkness in which to remain.

I remember being in that state, not realizing that the very reality for which I had been longing, the consummation for which my soul was hoping had been there since the moment of new birth, but I was never told that my seeking was to be with regard to an ever-present Christ. He is present and God desires to make His presence known so that they that glory would glory in the Lord who is present. 1 Corinthians 1:29 reads, *"That no flesh should glory in his presence."* The boasting of flesh, the assumption of the carnal man that he possesses a standing before God based upon self effort or observation is proof of ignorance with regard to the presence of Christ. The Greek word for the English phrase "in his presence" actually can and should be translated *"in the eye of God."*[79] I have been describing the eye of God; the Son upon whom the eye of God is eternally fixed; the exclusive perspective of the Father. However, only when our souls are unveiled to Christ are we made to comprehend how baseless any attempt to boast before God truly is.

That is why Paul writes in Philippians 3:4, *"Though I might also have confidence in the flesh. If any other man thinketh that he hath whereof he might trust in the flesh, I more."* If there was ever a man who could find room to boast in

---

[79] Robertson's Word Pictures in the New Testament, Electronic Database. Copyright © 1997, 2003, 2005, 2006 by Biblesoft, Inc. Robertson's Word Pictures in the New Testament. Copyright © 1985 by Broadman Press.

fleshly pursuits towards God, it would definitely be the Apostle Paul. But as we have said, Paul's heart had been judged; he stood in the eye of God, beholding substance and spiritual certainty. In that view, there was not ground upon which to boast except the solid and sufficient ground of the revealed presence of Christ. That is why after calling the zealous Jews the concision, he writes in Philippians 3:3, *"For we are the circumcision, which worship God in the Spirit, and rejoice in Christ Jesus, and have no confidence in the flesh."* His soul had been introduced to the New Covenant. Paul no longer boasted in a falsely assumed righteousness. Paul was beholding, in the eye of God, the only righteousness that exists, the righteousness that Christ is made unto the soul of every believer.

This is what I began to see. Why is it God's pleasure to reveal His Son in our souls? Remember, Paul prefaces this statement concerning God's pleasure to reveal His Son with his former manner of life under the Law. Within such a context, I realized that Paul was recalling all of his years, all of this time, all of his zealous pursuits toward God under the Law. He was looking back at everything he had done, every lesson he had learned at the feet of Gamaliel, and now as one living in the Light of the eye of God, Paul realizes that in every moment of every religious exercise, God had never been pleased. Is that not the very thing we read in Hebrews 10? Hebrews 10:6-8, *"In burnt offerings and sacrifices for sin thou hast had no pleasure. Then said I, Lo, I come (in the volume of the book it is written of me,) to do thy will, O God. Above when he said, Sacrifice and offering and burnt offerings and offering for sin thou wouldest not, neither hadst pleasure therein; which are offered by the Law."* God never found His satisfaction even in the things that gave testimony to the Person of His Satisfaction. His satisfaction was only realized in the coming of His Pleasure – Lo I come.... It is essential to understand that it is this coming (now in our hearts) wherein God's satisfaction is revealed and made known.

I remember a moment in Boone, North Carolina when this realization invaded my heart like the blasting of a trumpet. I went into a bedroom and I cried and repented and said, "God, forgive me because everything I have ever thought, every pursuit in which I have ever involved myself, every concept that I have ever had, and every word I have ever spoken has been wrong, it has been evil because it has been contrary to You." I meant that, but then I also vowed to Him, "Lord, I do not know anything, but I promise that if you will help me, if you will guide me in the realm of all Truth as you promised, I will never deviate my view from you." There is nothing else my friend. The soul demands and was created for this moment when God shows you His pleasure, the Son of his eternal satisfaction and utters in your soul - THIS IS HIM! Here is the moment for which your soul was created. and it must become a continuous moment if the New Covenant is ever to come into proper view.

So when Paul writes, "It pleased God to reveal His Son in Me," he is saying God was never pleased in anything I ever did. What a confession this is. This is a real confession of a soul that is beholding the One Pleasure of God and no longer living in the illusion that God has or will ever measure His satisfaction with man or his pursuits in view. The only answer to such illusion is the coming of Truth, the invasion of the Father's exclusive view. This has brought me to a greater understanding of Philippians 3:8, *"I count all things but loss for the excellency of the knowledge of Christ Jesus my Lord: for whom I have suffered the loss of all things, and do count them but dung, that I may win Christ."* I used to see this as a woeful declaration of loss and suffering. That is how we automatically read this, but I see it differently now. I see a man with his hands raised, a victorious smile on his face saying "Thank God, I have suffered the loss of all vain concepts; all self-centered and self-measured views of salvation in the revealed presence of the indwelling Christ. I have suffered the loss of darkness in the coming of the Light, I have suffered the loss of ignorance by the appearing of the eternal knowledge of God, I have suffered the loss of shadows in the coming of the substance." How in the world can that be a woeful declaration? How tremendous the transition that takes place by which the soul is capable of relinquishing what is of no value and lay hold upon Christ as the true gain and prosperity of the soul. It is tremendous to realize that the word "suffered" is actually in the passive tense here, which lets us know that this is not something we have to do; not a work we must perform and not a result of will power, but it is a work of God that takes place in us by the power and presence of another. It is the suffering or the taking away of the First through the inward establishing of the Second. That is the suffering. Paul is doubtlessly rejoicing in such a loss and we will as well! He is now beholding the more excellent One, the surpassing glory of Christ and he is rejoicing that he has suffered the loss and laid aside the weight and sin that easily besets the progress of the soul.[80]

That is a matter for true rejoicing. It is not a man crying out, "Oh God, I just hope I can pick up the pieces." He has realized that every piece and fragment has been gathered in Christ and those that were not gathered in Him, were never of Him and have been incinerated in the brightness of His

---

[80] Hebrews 12:1-2
Wherefore seeing we also are compassed about with so great a cloud of witnesses, let us lay aside every weight, and the sin which doth so easily beset us, and let us run with patience the race that is set before us, Looking unto Jesus the author and finisher of our faith…

coming. In Revelation 20:11 we read, *"And I saw a great white throne, and him that sat on it, from whose face the earth and the heaven fled away; and there was found <u>no place</u> for them."* That is referring to the first heaven and first earth; the Old Covenant. Again, this is not only applicable in a historical context, but that very encounter with the One on the throne also took place in Paul's heart. It must also happen in our hearts. In the countenance (revealed presence/face) of Him who sits upon His Throne, the first heaven and earth and the first man flees away, and there is no place found for them. Why? It is because HE fills up all things with Himself!

The word "place" in this verse does not just mean a span or an area, but it is limited by occupancy.[81] There was no place found for them because the true and rightful occupant of the land has come and now fills it with Himself! This takes place in the soul that truly beholds the One on the throne. The occupant for which the soul was created takes His rightful place, fills it with the knowledge of His fullness, and dispels all that does not have place where He is present. The New Covenant, our salvation, is defined by the occupancy of One. The same terminology is also used in Daniel 2:34-35, *"Thou sawest till that a stone was cut out without hands, which smote the image upon his feet that were of iron and clay, and brake them to pieces. Then was the iron, the clay, the brass, the silver, and the gold, broken to pieces together, and became like the chaff of the summer threshingfloors; and the wind carried them away, that no*

---

[81] NT:5117 τόπος topos (top'-os); apparently a primary word; a spot (general in space, but limited by occupancy; whereas NT:5561 is a large but participle locality), i.e. location (as a position, home, tract, etc.); figuratively, condition, opportunity; specifically, a scabbard. KJV - coast, licence, place, plain, quarter, rock, room, where. *(Biblesoft's New Exhaustive Strong's Numbers and Concordance with Expanded Greek-Hebrew Dictionary. Copyright © 1994, 2003, 2006 Biblesoft, Inc. and International Bible Translators, Inc.)*

place was found for them: and the stone that smote the image became a great mountain, and filled the whole earth." When the figure was smitten with the Stone, the image was destroyed and became as the chaff of the threshingfloors. It says beautifully that the wind carried them away. This is the wind of the Spirit, removing the false and destroyed image from the view of our hearts, so that no place is found for it at all. The Stone grows into a great mountain and fills the whole land with His increase. What a picture of the work of God in the heart that takes place when Christ (the Stone) is revealed. The Kingdom of God fills the land. There is no place now found for anything else. The One has occupied His place and now governs His land. I have faced this with every concept and image (imagination) that I had, in my ignorance, brought into Christ. In His face, every religious and zealous pursuit of our hearts becomes as chaff and there is no place found for it, thus leaving the soul with only one pursuit, which is to know Him.

In Philippians 3, Paul declares his soul's single pursuit in accordance with such an inward judgment – *"to know Him and be found in Him having nothing of my own."* See, that is the exclusivity of salvation. It comes to that. The Father desires to bring our hearts to this singleness of view. Paul writes, "God revealed His Son in me that I might preach HIM." Not preach the salvation of the New Covenant. No – preach HIM. Because He is the salvation of the New Covenant. In Him is everything in which God is well pleased. I want us to keep in mind what Paul is saying. All of his years learning, working zealously in pursuit of God, in all of it God never had pleasure. God never looked upon any of it and said, "I am well pleased." There is only One of whom and to whom God makes that declaration. That is what must happen inwardly. God must make known the exclusiveness of His view. The One who fills and in whom

God has summarized all things must be revealed in our hearts. Dear reader, the whole of God's pleasure and eternal delight now dwells in your heart. I can honestly say that God has no greater pleasure than to unveil the soul He has created to His own eternal satisfaction. That is the point. The inward revelation of Jesus Christ is the moment that God can finally show us His pleasure and make known satisfaction as it is defined in His eyes. That is when the New Covenant can truly become a subjective reality in the heart. Salvation cannot merely be an objective reality to which we have come, but it must become a subjective reality abounding within. In the Light of His presence, you now are liberated to experience the reality of newness of Life. But when it pleased God… this is the soul's transition into something altogether different, new, and perfect. Now God's pleasure is made known and you discover, it is not man to any degree, but is Christ who lives within.

May we consider this, submit our souls to the Father, so that He may reveal His good pleasure in us, and thereby free us from the deceptiveness of a self-measured or religiously defined view of salvation. It is my desire that we may all rejoice with Paul as those having suffered the loss of all else for the excellency of the knowledge of Christ Jesus our Lord.

CHAPTER FOUR

CHRIST IN YOU
THE FULFILLMENT OF ALL THINGS

As I write this chapter, we have lived through another failed prediction of the Day of the Lord's coming. I do not write that in order to make fun or make light of anyone, but in the light of what I will share in this chapter, it can be used as an object lesson. When these types of predictions are made and when people are so easily deceived to set their hopes upon such external happenings and events, my heart is grieved. This misplaced hope is due to what I understand to be a grave sense of dissatisfaction in the hearts of both those making and those believing these misguided guesses. When there is a working comprehension of the present Christ, such man created expectations will be understood to be without ground and unscriptural. Dear reader, the Light of the Day of the Lord's coming must be continually dawning and breaking forth in our hearts, or we will without a doubt long for a natural or supernatural day to come.

It is my conviction that our salvation can be encapsulated in the phrase, "Our God is faithful." This theme has reverberated in my soul for some time now, but with much greater emphasis than ever before. Unfortunately, when Christian religion speaks concerning God's faithfulness, it always seems to be defined with man and man's endeavors in view. By that, I mean that we attempt to make God faithful to things unto which He is not faithful. So then, to what is God faithful? God is faithful to that which He has always known and always desired. God is faithful to the One who eternally stood before His face as His daily delight and His pleasure. Moreover, His faithfulness is extended unto us in that He has brought us into a living union with that Son in whom His delight is realized.

The false expectations with which I started this chapter are derived from a misconception of God's faithfulness. The faithfulness of God is not defined by what God will one day do or what He promised He would do. The faithfulness of God is defined in one statement, "God has performed what He said He would do." Paul says this very thing in Acts 13 and in different places. Acts 13:32-33, *"And we declare unto you glad tidings, how that the promise which was made unto the fathers, God hath fulfilled* **the same** *unto us their children, in that he hath raised up Jesus again; as it is also written in the second psalm, Thou art my Son, this day have I begotten thee."* Any theology student worth his salt will admit that the promise mentioned here is all-encompassing. Within this phrase we face the totality of every promise and prophecy, as well as the One in whom all of those promises are yes and amen. We must also give diligence to the phrase "the same" in verse 33 because it definitely drives home the fact that God did not introduce a New Covenant that had different promises and intentions than the first. Every promise given unto the fathers throughout all the centuries prior to the Cross have come to their fulfillment in the Son God has raised out from among the dead. It seems like the term "fulfilled" should be very hard for us to misunderstand. It is the Greek word ekpleroo,[82] which means to accomplish entirely or to fill up completely. How can we have any type of longing for more when the salvation we have in the risen Son is without defect and lacking nothing at all with regard to completeness? The exact same promise given to the fathers is the exact same promise fulfilled and we are made partakers of that fulfilled promise by the indwelling presence of God's Son. There is nothing more and nothing different on God's agenda. In Christ, we have been given the fullness of the promise of God. Notice that Paul says he has fulfilled the same unto us their children. This has great significance for you and me. It means that Paul and those to whom he was speaking were already partaking of or had access to the fulfillment of God's promise. God's faithfulness is defined in these statements. I do not mean His faithfulness to get me a new car or His faithfulness to one day fulfill His promises. The faithfulness of God rings loud and clear: He hath fulfilled. His Son lives in me as the embodiment of His faithfulness. It would be a wonderful thing if our hearts were knowing in this present day, the fulfillment that Paul was knowing in his; instead of seeking a fulfillment that has no scriptural basis at all. However, for such discernment to be active in us, we must be living and walking in the Light of the revealed Son, as was Paul.

It seems that to speak of God's satisfaction, we must further look at that satisfaction and explore the reason the majority of Christians live in a state of dissatisfaction. When I think of this misplaced hope and the failed predictions that are not isolated to the latest, I understand that people are looking for fulfillment, for reality, and for consummation.

---

[82] NT:1603 ἐκπληρόω ekpleroo (ek-play-ro'-o); from NT:1537 and NT:4137; to accomplish entirely: KJV - fulfill. *(Biblesoft's New Exhaustive Strong's Numbers and Concordance with Expanded Greek-Hebrew Dictionary. Copyright © 1994, 2003, 2006 Biblesoft, Inc. and International Bible Translators, Inc.)*

However, they are seeking it in a realm in which it can never be discovered. That is because reality and fulfillment can only be found within the confines of one place and that is in Christ Himself. I am not referring to Christ as an abstract and theoretical concept, but Christ as He is in you. That is where fulfillment is found, that is where reality abides.

In the last chapter, I made an emphasis on Paul's phrase, *"But when it pleased God who separated me from my mother's womb and called me by His grace."* The emphasis was that Paul's soul was severed from all falsehood and empty religious zeal through being brought in reality and experience within the confines of Christ wherein all fullness is found. The severing or separation of which he writes is not what we think, but the separation of which he is referring has grace as its means and source. The definite separation that takes place objectively by grace comes into the soul as a subjective reality when the Son in whom we now abide, is revealed. When the grace of God dawns in our heart and we see what the grace of God has done, the soul can confess in understanding and in judgment, "Not I but Christ liveth in me," that is growing in grace and the knowledge of the Lord. Not I but Christ is the reality to which the grace of God has brought us; that is reality the moment you are born again, that is your state of being. That is not something that happens later on. That is a reality you come to the moment Christ indwells your soul. However, it is when the soul beholds that Son who lives within that the realization of that already present reality begins to dawn in the heart. Then it is not just a verse we read or a theme we quote; now it is a realty in the light of which we are living. That is what happened in Paul's heart.

I have stressed how important it was that Paul before saying, but when it pleased God to reveal His Son in me, began by looking at his time under the Law and under the elements of the Law. Now at one time in Paul's heart the Law was not a system of bondage, it was where he found his assumed righteousness. It is where he found and exercised himself in everything he thought God wanted. He thought that in doing those things he was pleasing God. Then Paul uses the phrase, *"but when it pleased God."* Yes, he was a devout Jew under that system; he excelled above his brethren because of his zeal toward that system. He was a man in the same condition as the Jews of whom he writes in Romans 10. He had zeal for God, yet without knowledge. He was ignorant of God's righteousness and utilized the Law in order to attempt to establish one of his own. Now by God's grace, by this tremendous work of grace, this man can write, "But when it pleased God." He is saying, all of those years, all of my life under that system, attempting to bring pleasure to God by obedience to external mandates and by involving myself in every religious observance possible, I had never pleased the God of my fathers. Not in one instance was God's pleasure found in his activities, because his activities were within the confines of a system in which God never found pleasure. That is perfectly said in Hebrews 10:8, *"Above when he said, Sacrifice and offering and burnt offerings and offering for sin thou wouldest not, neither hadst pleasure therein; which are offered by the Law."* God found no pleasure in them, how do you think He has pleasure in those who involve themselves in those things? Why did God not find pleasure in them? We will seek to answer that question in this chapter, but a simple answer, upon which I will expand, is that the testimony of reality can never bring satisfaction, only the coming of the substance of which the testimony spoke can. This is the answer given is it not: LO I COME! That not only is the answer historically, but it is more so the answer inwardly for the believer.

The testimony (which includes the Law and all of its elements) was a mere shadow, which gave an obscure outline of a Person, what Hebrews 10:1 calls the very image of the things. That image severed Paul's heart from zealous adherence to the shadows to an inward participation with the Substance. His heart came face to face with the very image of those external and representative things. The phrase, 'the very image of the things' speaks of the eternal Substance that stood before the Father and was the basis of every testimonial element unto which Paul had wholly given himself. His soul encountered the origin of all things. That is a soul-transitioning, soul-transforming view that only comes in the revelation of the Son. It is only through that Spirit given encounter that the soul comes to know and experience fulfillment. Fulfillment is never found in external things. Fulfillment is never found in things seen. Fulfillment is only discovered when the unseen reality dawns in our hearts. The fact is that fulfillment already abides in us because Christ is already there. However, our souls do not know the fulfillment until we see, until our hearts are unveiled to the fulfillment that God has already provided. It is to this that God is faithful. Not only has He been faithful to fulfill His promise, but He is equally faithful to reveal the fulfillment of the promise He has given to us.

In verse 22 of Hebrews 10, we then read, *"Let us draw near with a true heart in full assurance of faith, having our hearts sprinkled from an evil conscience."* At this time, I will not go deep into the meaning here because we will deal with the conscience in an upcoming chapter. However, I will just mention that an evil conscience is a conscience or a comprehension of salvation that is still looking and seeking within the elements of the Law; an understanding of salvation that is joined to and still seeking within that to which God no longer relates, in an attempt to find fulfillment. Unfortunately, while our hearts are seeking in a realm of vain shadows, we will find a way to convince ourselves that those shadows have substance to them. We are easily convinced when we want to be. We can be easily convinced that better things are coming one day when we are not seeing the Better One who has come and now inhabits the soul.

That is why Paul continually warns them, do not allow this to happen, do not entertain the foolish babblings of people. Therefore, in Hebrews 10:23 we read, *"Let us hold fast the profession of our faith without wavering...."* What is the ground for such a holding fast, such an unwavering of heart? Upon what basis can that be done? **"For he is faithful that promised."** You have to see this statement within the context of this letter and even this chapter; lo, I come to do thy will.... How is that defined? He takes away the First and establishes the Second; that is something He did. It is in view of this finished work that Paul says to these being forced and deceived into looking back at the thing Christ has put away; hold fast your profession of faith without wavering. He is saying the same thing to the Colossians. Colossians 1:23, *"...Be not moved away from the hope of the gospel, which ye have heard, and which was preached to every creature which is under heaven; whereof I Paul am made a minister."* Colossians 2:8, *"Beware lest any man spoil you through philosophy and vain deceit, after the tradition of men, after the rudiments of the world, and not after Christ."* Let no man cause you to seek reality and fullness within these types and figures; they are merely a shadow; they have no substance to them; the Substance has come, and He is in you. Not only does he write that but in Colossians 3:1-2 he writes, *"If ye then be risen with Christ, seek those things which are above, where Christ sitteth on the right hand of God. Set your affection on things above, not on things on the earth."* Seeing that you are risen or brought into a union with this One who is the substance and the very image of those things, no longer look to the earth, no longer seek within the confines of these external things to discover spiritual reality and fulfillment, set your affection on an above reality. Set your affection in the heavens where Christ sitteth. Our souls are in union with fulfillment, the very image of the shadows Himself. In view of that, why would we ever look to the things that were merely shadows? That question is simple to answer. It is because, to the majority of us, they are not shadows at all. In our natural comprehension, they are substantial and concrete. That is due to blindness of heart, meaning we have not and are not beholding the real thing. Until reality dawns in the heart, the other seems authentic. The natural mind measures reality by such criteria as it is tangible and it is outwardly observable. Because of this, I often consider what a tremendous transition must have taken place in Paul's heart. This man, who was so devout to these external things (circumcision, feasts, etc.), could now look at those same elements, still present and functioning, and call them nothing but mere shadows. It is important enough to repeat that God did not tear down the temple before or when He revealed Christ in the heart of Paul. Those things were still visible to the natural faculties and vast multitudes thought they were still authorized by God. Nevertheless, Paul observed those same outward things and in his heart knew they possessed nothing of spiritual reality and to hold to them and set the heart within those things was a perversion. No matter how impressive the edifices and trappings of that system were or how fascinating they were, they were not valid. That is something we as Christians must really consider. Naturally impressive does not mean spiritually relevant. Paul came to see the nothingness of all those things when he saw the real thing revealed in the face of the indwelling Christ. That revelation brings a separation, an inward severing. In the

Light of that judgment, Paul preached the gospel and the gospel forbids any external thing to be given spiritual validity at all. I am not saying that we should not do things that are seen. I am saying that seen things are never the evidence of reality. The external, during the testimony, as well as present day, never constitutes the proof of fulfillment and Truth.

Reality has never been defined in events or in any other external manifestations. Fulfillment and reality have always been defined in an unseen source, in an origin that man could never see, but that was exclusively God's perspective. It was exclusively His. We are going to explore that as we proceed in this chapter. Paul could look at these things and now say they are merely shadows. They have no substance to them. Paul worked, slaved, and labored under this system and we do the same thing. We seek reality in the coming of events; we seek reality and fulfillment in external manifestations and religious observances. We will never find satisfaction there and the soul will never know fulfillment there. Just like Paul, we will never find what our souls are truly longing for in any of the seen things.

The soul was created by God for reality. Why is it that our souls cannot be satisfied in those external things? It is simply because God was never satisfied in those things. Therefore, if God created your soul, is it not at least reasonable that your soul cannot be satisfied with something less than the very thing that satisfies God's heart? This is very difficult for most to accept, but there has never been anything seen that has pleased God. You and I are especially included in that statement. God has created the soul of man therefore, it is impossible for that soul to experience satisfaction and fulfillment except in the light of, or the revealed presence of, God's own satisfaction.

In one of our previous chapters, I defined salvation as our souls being permitted into a participation with a satisfied God by union with Christ who is His satisfaction. Unfortunately, most people who have been permitted into such a participation have no idea what that means. I thank God because He has always dealt with humanity in view of a satisfaction He already possesses. I tell God continually, "Thank you for not dealing with me according to my ignorance but according to your eternal knowledge. Now let that knowledge become the Light in which I live."

Trying to be God's pleasure, trying to be God's satisfaction is a torturous cycle. Some days you convince yourself you are and the next day you know you are not. I talk to people who are having that struggle. One brother recently told me that when people look at him they want to see Jesus. In all honesty, I told him that their expectation is misplaced. They are never going to see Jesus in you. That is true. He then wanted to know what it was they were to see. The answer is that they must turn their heart's attention and see Jesus for themselves. They will never observe spiritual evidence in the face and actions of any human being. Therefore, when they see us, they see a man or a woman living in the inward acknowledgment of the revealed Christ. That is what they see. The moment someone deceives themselves into thinking they are going to see Jesus in a person, they have diverted the attention of their heart away from reality. Now you are looking at me or someone else for something you will never find there, just like looking in the earth for events that are never going to happen. They have to see Jesus the same way you have to see Jesus. God must reveal His Son in their hearts. That is the only way. So what do I do as a believer? I declare the Christ I am knowing. I declare to them the Christ I am seeing, whether one on one or in a group. I declare Him and the necessity of their souls being unveiled to Him. As a believer, I live in the acknowledgement of reality every day and speak to them out from that reality so that maybe their hearts would have a hunger birthed inside to turn and see the same Jesus I am seeing. Again, people seek reality in man or in cunningly devised fables because the soul of man is always seeking the reality for which it was created; but the soul cannot be satisfied with something less than God's own satisfaction because God created the soul. The grace of God, the love of God toward us is that He desires for His joy, His satisfaction to be made full or to abound in us.

Let us now continue our consideration of Hebrews 10:1, *"For the Law having a shadow of good things to come, and not the very image of the things...."* The phrase "good things to come" does not refer to unfulfilled elements that were yet to come when the Hebrew letter was being written. Under the Law, the good things were still yet to come. The Law was a shadow of the good things to come because it testified of the Good One to come. I must now focus on this phrase, "not the very image of the things." Notice how it is worded, "the very image (singular) of the things (plural)." There was a time when the various representational elements, which were given of God for a testimony of His Son, had validity, but they were never the end in and of themselves. There was always "the very image of those things" that stood behind it all as their source and basis for existing. These testimonial elements were a shadow but there was a Body, as it says in Colossians,[83] which eternally existed as the Father's view. That eternal Body cast upon the earth the shadow that we call the testimony.

---

[83] Colossians 2:16-17
Let no man therefore judge you in meat, or in drink, or in respect of an holyday, or of the new moon, or of the sabbath days: Which are a shadow of things to come; but the body is of Christ.

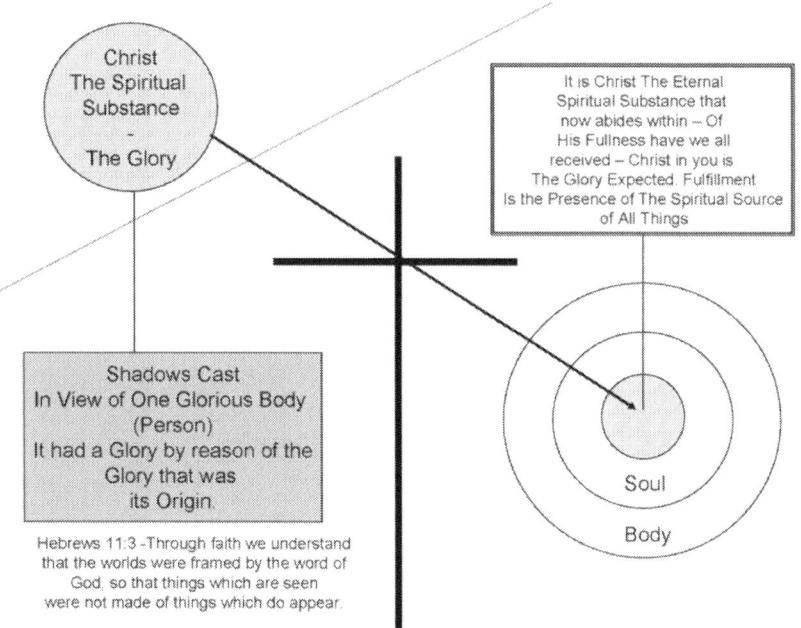

The diagram above illustrates that very thing. The shadows were cast by a Glorious Body, a Glorious Substance who was before any of those things were created. You may recall verses such as, John 1:15, *"John bare witness of him, and cried, saying, This was he of whom I spake, He that cometh after me is preferred **before** me: for he was before me."* John 8:58, *"Jesus said unto them, Verily, verily, I say unto you, **Before** Abraham was, I am."* Therefore, in an inward view of this One who was "before," the writer can say of the elements of that testimony, they are <u>not the very image</u> and that is important to keep in mind as we continue. The soul cannot be satisfied in the things. The soul will only be satisfied in the **revealed presence of the very image of those things**. While it is true that we cannot experience this inward discernment until Christ is revealed, the majority of Christians today do not even understand it scripturally. All I can do in this book is present it scripturally. God will have to do the rest, but that will only take place when the heart tires of holding to the "things"

and cries out for God to reveal the very image of those things. The burden that I continually bear is that, although our God is satisfied, the majority of his people are not, and because of this, they are vainly seeking that satisfaction in the realm of external elements. That is why I am stressing that we cannot be satisfied; we cannot experience satisfaction in any of the external outward things because they were not and are not what satisfied God's heart. There is a huge difference between fascination and satisfaction. There is a difference between pacification and satisfaction. By that, I mean people can be fascinated by religious things, outward manifestations, and people falling on the floor, or events that may happen one day. That is fascinating to many. It is entertaining. My late brother in law, who I considered as my natural brother, called those things spiritual entertainment. These things anesthetize our souls and divert our attention from what is truly beneficial.

Paul says that very thing in Galatians 3:1, *"O foolish Galatians, who hath bewitched you...."* Interestingly, the word "bewitched" in the Greek also means, "to fascinate by false representation."[84] Their hearts were being fascinated with the elements of the testimony, diverting their hearts from the Truth Himself. This fascination was truly about looking into the earth and attempting to find in flesh, in religion, in outward observations that which is solely

---

[84] NT:940 βασκαίνω baskaino (bas-kah'-ee-no); akin to NT:5335; to malign, i.e. (by extension) to fascinate (by false representations): KJV - bewitch.

NT:940
1. baskaino (βασκαίνω, NT:940), primarily, "to slander, to prate about anyone"; then "to bring evil on a person by feigned praise, or mislead by an evil eye, and so to charm, bewitch" (Eng., "fascinate" is connected), is used figuratively in Galatians 3:1, of leading into evil doctrine. *(Vine's Expository Dictionary of Biblical Words, Copyright © 1985, Thomas Nelson Publishers.)*

experienced in the revealed presence of Christ. That is a bewitching and a fascination that is running rampant in the Christian religion today. Have you been fascinated or is your soul looking in the face of God's own satisfaction, and therein finding your satisfaction? The Galatians were being fascinated and fascination can hold you for a short or long period. You can be fascinated by these things but that is not satisfaction. You can even be pacified by these things, but that is not satisfaction. Religious pacification and fascination will divert your attention and the affection of your heart toward a false object and cause you to be involved in what I call a "false vocation." The vocation given to us by God in Christ is exclusively to know Christ, to know the Lord, to see Christ and to grow up in the knowledge of Him. The other will divert your attention to see things, to know things, and to get involved in some religious activities that are detrimental to spiritual growth. Such diverts your heart. It is detrimental to your soul. I did not say that you would go to hell. I am saying that in a state of such distraction you will not know or experience the Life that you have been given by God. You will not know the present indwelling fulfillment. Who has fascinated you?

I am presenting you with true satisfaction. I want to over emphasize that there is only One who can satisfy the soul that God created because God created it to be filled with His own satisfaction. With regard to salvation, satisfaction is not something that is individually defined. That means that the satisfaction of my soul can in no way differ from yours. That means, with regard to salvation, I cannot be satisfied with something and you be satisfied with something else. The soul I am and the soul you are will only be satisfied with that One Substance for which God Himself has created it. That Substance is His Son.

The things of the testimony were a shadow of the good things to come. [85] *The Exegetical Dictionary of the New Testament* gives the following as its definition. *"Skia can refer to the shadow of an object and hence a mere copy, in contrast to the reality or true and essential being."* I like that they used the word being. There is a True and Essential Being that lies as the source of that shadow. In fact, the Essential Being is the Truth. Remember the Greek definition of Truth I sited earlier in this book. It is *"the reality, which lies as the basis of an appearance or the basis of what appears."* Adam Clark writes, *"The very image is the model or substance according to which anything is formed."* When I read the word "formed," I went back to different verses in the Old Testament where God is dealing with the types and the figures, especially with Israel, but even man himself. God formed man of the dust of the earth. How did He and why did He form man? What was the source of that? It was done out from and in view of an Essential Being. Just consider these verses, Isaiah 43:1, *"But now thus saith the Lord that created thee, O Jacob, and he that formed thee, O Israel, Fear not: for I have redeemed thee, I have called thee by thy name; thou art mine."* Isaiah 43:7, *"Even every one that is called by my name: for I have created him for my glory, I have formed him; yea, I have made him."* God formed it but He formed it in view of the very image Himself. Israel is my Son. How could He say that? He can say that because there was a Son before His face when He made that declaration. [86]

---

[85] NT:4639 σκία skia (skee'-ah); apparently a primary word; "shade" or a shadow (literally or figuratively [darkness of error or an adumbration]): KJV - shadow. *(Biblesoft's New Exhaustive Strong's Numbers and Concordance with Expanded Greek-Hebrew Dictionary. Copyright © 1994, 2003, 2006 Biblesoft, Inc. and International Bible Translators, Inc.)*

[86] Exodus 4:22
And thou shalt say unto Pharaoh, Thus saith the Lord, Israel is my son, even my firstborn.

One commentary says that it speaks of something formed as a potter forms a vessel, so I went back to the potter in Jeremiah 18. Jeremiah 18:3-4, *"Then I went down to the potter's house, and, behold, he wrought a work on the wheels. And the vessel that he made of clay was marred in the hand of the potter: so he made it again another vessel, as seemed good to the potter to make it."* Remember, there are two vessels and one potter. In reality, these vessels speak of two covenants, two administrations. In this depiction, you see the contrast between the first and the second. The first vessel is made of clay and Jeremiah is very careful to state that it was made of clay when describing the first vessel. He does not state that when referring to the second vessel. The first is made of clay and it was marred in the hands of the potter. The potter, without a doubt created it. He was definitely the originator and source of that vessel. However, it was now in a state of ruin, it was in an irreversible state of defect and deficiency.[87]

We just looked at Hebrews 10 and in it we were made aware of the defect, *"it could not bring the comers thereunto perfection."* Here is the fatal flaw of that system. Hebrews 8:7, *"For if that first Covenant had been free from imperfection, there would have been no attempt to introduce another."*[88] That is what these vessels represent. There is a defective system and then there is the introduction of ANOTHER, which is not another system of Laws and observances to be applied to clay vessels, but is the Son of God, the Lord from Heaven, who is the full and

---

[87] shachat OT:7843, "to corrupt, spoil, ruin, mar, destroy." *(Vine's Expository Dictionary of Biblical Words, Copyright © 1985, Thomas Nelson Publishers.)*

[88] Weymouth New Testament

perfect intention of the Father living in the soul of man. The term "another" in the above translation is "the second" in the King James. The actual Greek word is "deuteros," which means second or afterwards. When you read the scripture and the terms "second" and "afterwards" are used, they usually refer to the New Covenant, the spiritual reality that is come and is embodied in Christ. If the first covenant had been free of imperfection, then there would have been no attempt to introduce another. The fact is, the potter had an intention in his mind and in view of that intention, he created a vessel. That first vessel did not fulfill his expectation; it did not fulfill his intention. This needs to be addressed. What was the flaw in the first? The most succinct answer I can give is, it was not Christ.

In view of the defect that kept this vessel from meeting the potter's intention, Jeremiah goes on and says that the potter made it **again another vessel**. When most read this, they think that it speaks of a remaking of the first, but it is not a remaking of the first vessel. We also think that salvation is the remaking and perfecting of the First. It is not. The term "another" in the Hebrew can mean "different."[89] He sought for "another" because the first was imperfect in that it did not fulfill His intent from the beginning. He, therefore, made an altogether other, altogether different, altogether new vessel. Here is the key statement that shows the difference between these two vessels or covenants, *"as it seemed good to the potter or as it pleased Him to make it."* He had an original intention. In His mind, He knew what He was after. He had an original intention. Carefully consider this; He had a predetermined intention. Does that bring any verses into your mind?[90] He had already

---

[89] OT:312 acher OT:312, "following; different; other." *(Vine's Expository Dictionary of Biblical Words, Copyright © 1985, Thomas Nelson Publishers.)*

[90] Ephesians 1:5

predetermined that which would satisfy Him. If you look at this in the perspective of the Heavenly Potter, it makes perfect sense. Both vessels were formed by the one Potter. The first testified of an intention but it was not the fullness that was intended. God's pleasure is exclusive to the Son that stood before Him and the only thing that fulfilled His eternal intention was the coming of that Son. Unlike the potter in Jeremiah, the Father did not merely have a picture in His mind of what it would look like; He eternally had the substance and fulfillment of that intention before His face. What was the flaw of the first? **It was not the very image**. It was not what He intended. Yes, it testified, it was a prophecy of "another" to come. That first vessel was a prophecy of another vessel that was going to come, the coming of which would fully please the Potter.

We have to understand that fulfillment is not God bringing in more shadows, it is not more things that are external. That is what the majority of Christians suppose fulfillment will be. They say that we have a partial salvation at present, until this external, physical thing happens to bring about consummation. In reality, the thing seen, the external testimony, was always **unto** the coming of the spiritual reality. *"But that which is spiritual [is] not first, but that which [was] natural,* ***afterwards that which [is] Spiritual.***"[91] Fulfillment is never found in natural things, then or now. I reiterate that fulfillment was never things that had to happen, but someone who had to come.

Having predestinated us unto the adoption of children by Jesus Christ to himself, according to the good pleasure of his will.

Ephesians 1:11
In whom also we have obtained an inheritance, being predestinated according to the purpose of him who worketh all things after the counsel of his own will.

[91] 1 Corinthians 15:46 – Young's Literal Translation

Fulfillment was not found in the external testimony given of God, therefore it is definitely not found in the external things that have been invented in the darkened hearts of religious men. Fulfillment has always been the Son that perpetually stands before the Father. What is fulfillment presently? **Fulfillment is that same Son now living in you.** That is why I wrote earlier that such false predictions are a perfect example, because people are now looking for something more to come because they are ignorant of the indwelling Christ, the very thing that was always expected and the very image unto which the shadows pointed. They may be informed of the fact that He does dwell in them, but they remain ignorant of Him who indwells. I state it that way because it is possible to believe that He indwells you and still live with a false expectation of the coming of something more. Yet, when your soul is unveiled to the Son in His Presence and you behold in His face the I AM of God, there is no "place or room" remaining for any such false expectations because He fulfills the expectation of the soul.

As you can see in the previous diagram, I have written "Glory" in three specific places. Paul would say in 2 Corinthians 3:10, *"For even that which was made glorious had no glory in this respect, by reason of the glory that excelleth."* That system (Law, Testimony) had a glory given to it. It says specifically, it was **made** glorious. What does that mean? It was lent a glory. It did not have a glory of its own. Remember, it was a shadow, it was empty and without substance. It did not have glory of its own; it was given a glory by God. God lent it a glory. What glory? It had a glory because there was a greater glory that stood as its origin, as its source. Israel saw clouds, they saw smoke, they saw fire, they saw all of those things, but they were still shut out as to the knowledge of the Truth and meaning of which those external things testified. Unfortunately, there are Christians today that desire to see those very things manifest in their midst. They would fall on their faces if a cloud of glowing smoke and fire were to materialize in the middle of the room. They desire to see the externals because that is what is real to them. That is real to them because they have not seen the very image, the Essential Being according to which all testimonial elements were formed. Those things had an unseen and spiritual origin. Fulfillment for us is the appearing and the presence of that unseen reality in the soul. It is very simple. What is real is that which is Spirit and Truth, not what is tangible, external, and outward. God testified and prophesied of a time in which He would reveal His satisfaction. He did that historically, but that also must be taking place presently in the soul of every believer. He must be revealed in the soul that was created to be the habitation of God's satisfaction. God would make that satisfaction known in us. Why? It is because Christ is not only the fulfillment we have desired, but also He is the fulfillment that God has always beheld before Him.

Neither the prophets nor the types and the shadows were testifying of contingent events. God did not make predictions, which were contingent upon the coming of future events, because the Father sees and declares the End from the Beginning. His comprehension and eternal knowledge is exclusively defined in the face of His Son who is the Beginning and the End. Isaiah 46:9-10, *"Remember the former things of old: for I am God, and there is none else; I am God, and there is none like me, Declaring the end from the beginning, and from ancient times the things that are not yet done, saying, My counsel shall stand, and I will do all my pleasure."* How did He see from the beginning, an end that had not yet happened? That is not how God sees. God's End and His Beginning is the eternal Son. God does not abide by a linear timeline.

The End and Beginning in the Father's view is the Being of His Son. Jesus says, *"I am the beginning and the end."*[92] He is talking with regard to God's eternal purpose, plan, and original intention. "I Am the Alpha and the Omega," which conveys to us that within the confines of His Person, all eternal reality is found. The Beginning and The End are One.

The fulfillment we possess in Christ is the same one God always had in view. Barnes Notes reads, *"They (the prophets) didn't testify of contingent events or happenings that were dependent upon unknown factors. The basis of every prophetic utterance that was given, had a fixed and a settled substance."* The basis of every prophetic utterance in the testimony had a fixed and a settled substance. That is why I wrote earlier, God never worked toward a goal. God never worked to fulfill something He did not already possess. God always worked and now works in our hearts in view of the Goal, the End that was always before His face. The reality and substance that Christ is was never to be fulfilled but was to be revealed. The elements that testified of Him were fulfilled but only in His revealing, in His coming. That is so because He was their source. God was not making things up as He went along. God had an original intention and a fountainhead out from which He did and said all that He did and said. We read in Hebrews 1:1-2, *"In many parts and in different ways God in former times having spoken to the fathers by means of the prophets, in the last of these days spoke to us in One who by nature is [His] Son, whom He appointed heir of all things,* **through whom also He constituted the ages**.*"*[93]

---

[92] Revelation 1:8, 3:14, 21:6

[93] The New Testament: An Expanded Translation by Kenneth S. Wuest Copyright © 1961 by Wm. B. Eerdmans Publishing Co. All rights reserved

What brought those days of prophecy and the age of testimony to their conclusion? Was it an event? It was not according to this verse. The conclusion and fulfillment of those days was the revealing, the coming of the Son who was daily His delight and was His view before anything that was made was made.[94] Now that is historically true but more so for us, it is inwardly true and necessary. The coming of the Son brings all testimony and prophecy to their intended End because in His inward revealing, we come face to face with the Person who is their source and consummation. Also, notice this very important phrase, "through whom also He constituted the ages." That will be important as we proceed.

Christ was the source and eternal substance of all things seen and prophesied, that is why Peter can say that no prophet spoke according to his own private interpretation. 2 Peter 1:19, *"Knowing this first, that every prophecy of scripture does not originate from any private explanation [held by the writer], for not by the desire of man did prophecy come aforetime, but being carried along by the Holy Spirit men spoke words from God who is the ultimate*

---

[94] Proverbs 8:22-30
The Lord possessed me in the beginning of his way, before his works of old. I was set up from everlasting, from the beginning, or ever the earth was. When there were no depths, I was brought forth; when there were no fountains abounding with water. Before the mountains were settled, before the hills was I brought forth: While as yet he had not made the earth, nor the fields, nor the highest part of the dust of the world. When he prepared the heavens, I was there: when he set a compass upon the face of the depth: When he established the clouds above: when he strengthened the fountains of the deep: When he gave to the sea his decree, that the waters should not pass his commandment: when he appointed the foundations of the earth: Then I was by him, as one brought up with him: and I was daily his delight, rejoicing always before him.

source [of what they spoke]."[95] If it is true that no private interpretation was permitted with regard to the prophetic declarations of the old, it is unquestionably true concerning our comprehending of the reality and fullness of those prophetic words. When our hearts behold the source of all things, the Essential Being and meaning in view of which all things were made and all prophecies were given. Such a work leaves no room for our private considerations.

This will be clearer when we look at John chapter 1. Before we go there, it is necessary to consider a far too often overlooked and misunderstood verse in Hebrews chapter 11. This will set the stage for John 1. Hebrews 11:3, *"Through faith we understand that the worlds were framed by the word of God, so that things which are seen were not made of things which do appear."* I believe Mr. Wuest to have the better translation of this verse. It reads, *"By means of faith we perceive that the material universe and **the God-appointed ages of time** were equipped and fitted by God's word for the purpose for which they were intended, and it follows therefore that that which we see did not come into being out of that which is visible."* Through faith, we understand that the worlds were framed by the word of God. In the beginning was the Word.... This is where we are going. I love how Mr. Wuest not only relates this to the material universe, but the God appointed ages (or the age of testimony that was appointed unto the coming of the Son). The "things which are seen" in this verse relate to the God appointed age of the Old Covenant. As I have been stating, that age consisted of a multitude of outwardly evident and naturally observed elements. However, those observable elements existed as one God ordained testimony of an

---

[95] The New Testament: An Expanded Translation by Kenneth S. Wuest Copyright © 1961 by Wm. B. Eerdmans Publishing Co. All rights reserved.

eternal Son that could never be and will never be observed except by the seeing of faith. Therefore, He prefaces these statements by writing, "by faith we understand...." Contrary to the most common definition of faith, it is actually a means of comprehending spiritual reality, it is actually spiritual reality revealed and at work in our hearts. If we are not understanding by faith, we are attempting to understand and thereby are misunderstanding spiritual things by natural means such as intellect.

Again, the things that are seen are the things of the testimony. That is the point of this letter. He is attempting to bring them from the external testimony to the inward revealed Witness of that testimony. That is why this writer implores them in Hebrews 6:1, *"Therefore, having put away once for all the beginning word of the Messiah [the first testament in animal blood, i.e., the Mosaic economy], let us be carried along to that which is complete [the new testament in Jesus' blood."*[96]

The writer is making known that the source and origin of the visible things of that age was not observable or natural. They had a heavenly, unseen, and spiritual origin, so the fulfillment of these things that were seen cannot be more things that are seen. The fulfillment of a blueprint cannot be another blueprint. The fulfillment of a blueprint is the complete house that was in the mind of the architect and was the source of the blueprint being drafted. Fulfillment is the coming of the source and summation Himself and glory be to the Grace of God, that coming takes place in us. He appears in the soul as the end, the goal of all things and as the satisfaction of the Father's heart, thereby the soul

---

[96] The New Testament: An Expanded Translation by Kenneth S. Wuest Copyright © 1961 by Wm. B. Eerdmans Publishing Co. All rights reserved.

experiences the satisfaction for which it exists. Does that mean that we no longer care about anything and say, "to hell with the world, we have ours?" No, satisfaction does not mean that at all. Satisfaction means that we have found what we have longed for, we have found the reason we exist and now we set our affection to discover the eternal dimensions and riches of the Life we have found. It also motivates us to declare Him to whomever we find who has a hungry heart, so that they may experience the same satisfaction.

Hebrews 11 again reads that the worlds were framed by the Word of God. The term "framed" in the Greek means to be put in a complete and perfect order. [97] The material universe and the God appointed ages of time were equipped and fitted by God's word for the purpose for which they were intended. That is why it is tremendous that the word for "world" in Hebrews 11:3 is actually "aion," which actually speaks of the age of promise.[98] There can be no doubt that we are being presented here with the external age of testimony. That age was framed and equipped for the purpose for which it was intended. But when was the purpose fulfilled? Their time was fulfilled with the appearing of the Very Image of those things. Now the question must be asked. When are those seen things no longer necessary and when do they no longer possess validity in the heart? They no longer have legitimacy in us when the Very Image of the things appears in us. So Paul can say, as a man who has been separated unto and

---

[97] NT:2675 καταρτίζω katartizœ put (again) into order,
(from Exegetical Dictionary of the New Testament © 1990 by William B. Eerdmans Publishing Company. All rights reserved.)

[98] NT:165 αἰών aion (ahee-ohn'); from the same as NT:104; properly, an age; by extension, perpetuity (also past); by implication, the world; specially (Jewish) a Messianic period (present or future)

confined within the borders of spiritual reality, "we look not at the things that are seen but the things that are unseen." That is truly living by faith and not by sight. We must understand that faith does not hope for unseen things until they manifest into seen things. Faith beholds spiritual substance, which cannot be observed any other way. Faith is the spiritual faculty that beholds the revealed Christ as the substance and the evidence that was expected yet unseen; but faith sees that evidence and substance to be Christ within. That is why it is by faith that we understand that the external things of the age of testimony were framed and given their existence by a spiritual source. If faith is not the sight and understanding in and by which we walk, we will observe natural things and call them real because of their availability to the natural mind. Faith beholds the spiritual source of all things as a present indwelling reality, thus inwardly defining fulfillment.

Now back to John chapter 1. John 1:1-3, *"In the beginning was the Word, and the Word was with God, and the Word was God. The same was in the beginning with God. All things were made by him; and without him was not any thing made that was made."* Do you see the connection with Hebrews 11:3, because it is here we are brought to see the unseen Source and Eternal Word by which the worlds were framed. *"All things were made by Him and without Him* (or outside of His Divine Person) *was not anything made that was made."* Here we see the Very Image of the things.

We now go to verses 14-16, *"And the Word was made flesh, and dwelt among us, (and we beheld his glory, the glory as of the only begotten of the Father,) full of grace and truth. John bare witness of him, and cried, saying, This was he of whom I spake, He that cometh after me is preferred before me: for he was before me. And of his fulness have all we received, and grace for grace."* John was witness of this One. Remember that in John the Baptist we observe the summation of the testimony of both the Law and Prophets. John's life was a testimony of the coming of "Another." John 1:15, *"He that cometh **after** me is preferred before me: for he was before me."* Here is a beautiful summation of the life and ministry of John as well as a perfect heading for the whole of the age of testimony. John 1:19-20, *"And this is the record of John, when the Jews sent priests and Levites from Jerusalem to ask him, Who art thou? And he confessed, and denied not; but confessed, I am not the Christ."* That is the great declaration summing up the testimony, the seen things: I am not the Christ. This was the flaw of that vessel, that system. Why did John have to decrease through the increase of the One that comes after? In a statement, "I'm not him. I am not the Christ." Why could Ishmael not remain? It was simply because He was not Isaac. Why can the first no longer stand and possess validity? It is not the Second.

Here is the point I want you to understand and appreciate. John 1:16, *"And **of his fulness have all we received**, and grace for grace."* Wuest reads, *"for out of His fulness as a source we all received."* Consider this with me. Whose fullness have we received? Whose fullness and substance do we presently possess as born again believers? I knew this scripturally. I knew this doctrinally. However, when you see it from John's perspective and the eternal perspective presented in John 1:1-3, the significance is amazing. He was the source, the predicate upon which John's life and the testimony he represented was based. We now have residing in our hearts the Substance, Life, and Fullness of that Eternal Origin and Meaning of all things. What a salvation. This is our salvation. The source Himself, the origin, the original intention of God, now resides in our souls. We have His fullness, Him as fullness, Him as fulfillment living in us. Of His fullness, have all we received. John 1:17, *"For the Law was given by Moses, but grace and truth came by Jesus Christ."* I love the wording here. The Law was **given** by Moses (but that Law had a spiritual source). The Law was given by Moses, but grace and truth **came**. Grace and Truth; the spiritual nature and essence of which the Law spoke but could not provide, **came in and as Christ**. How wonderful it is to know in the Light of His revealed presence that of His fullness we have all received. Fulfillment and eternal evidence will NEVER be found in the things seen, whether things of the Old Covenant or the things seen in our day and time to which we give false validity. Reality is embodied in Christ and experienced in Christ revealed.

God desires that all souls in whom such fullness resides would come to be enraptured, caught away, and totally confined in an internal realization within the realm of eternal fulfillment. However, that will never happen in the soul of the one who still looks for reality in the realm of seen things. That is why there is the necessity of the turning of the heart from what is seen to what cannot be seen. When that is the posture, the heart is in absolute dependence upon God to reveal what is exclusively His view. We cannot see it or touch it naturally and that makes it impossible to corrupt. So many people get offended when they are presented with just how "spiritual" the Second really is. All things of this creation and covenant in Christ are OF GOD and NOT OF US. That is fulfillment. Fulfillment is the indwelling and revealing of the Spiritual, Perfect, Incorruptible Christ who is God's eternal satisfaction. Let us set the affection of our souls upon the knowing of Him as fulfillment and cease seeking for it where it can never be found. May we cease looking for consummation in events, or being fascinated by outward things or being pacified by momentary ecstasies, but may we be those who are living in a perpetual state of satisfaction in the Light of the knowledge of the Glory of God in the face of Jesus Christ. This is my prayer for the Body of Christ. I desire that we all live daily in a God given view of fulfillment. That is how Paul, at one time a zealous Jew, could go forth declaring an altogether other. He went declaring "another" Covenant, "another" House, "another" Law, and "another" Man. His heart was no longer constrained to what was flawed and deficient. His soul was beholding Another who pleases the Father. If we are to live in the good of our salvation, we must come face to face with the Very Image of the things. May we be those who live in an uninterrupted view of Christ our fulfillment.

Think of this in relation to the Word who was in the beginning, even the Word in view of whom and by whom all things were made. Oh, the faithfulness of our God that has made it possible for these words to be penned with regard to that eternal source and origin – of His Fullness **Have All We Received**. It is the One Who was in the Beginning being resident and being revealed in our souls. Fulfillment and fullness is a reality from the moment of His coming to dwell within. However, we begin to comprehend Him as fulfillment when our souls are unveiled to His presence. That is knowing and experiencing fulfillment as from the beginning. That is our salvation: of His fullness have all we received. Salvation is fulfillment. It is not waiting for it, but being indwelt by the Person of fulfillment Himself. That is why we must not look for fulfillment anywhere other than the Christ of God who abides within.

That is why it is by faith that we comprehend that the seen things have unseen and eternal origin, because if faith is not the dominating vision and view of our hearts, we will look at tangible and outwardly observable things and call them real. God desires to unveil our souls to the only thing that is real. We have come to the mountain that cannot be touched. This speaks to the fact that what we have come to in Christ is the unseen fullness that was always expected. It is not touchable or temporal, but eternal in the Person of the indwelling Son of God. It must be understood also that this matter of fulfillment does not only pertain to the Old Covenant elements, so let me ask this question in summation. Where do you look for the fulfillment and full measure of righteousness, love, or holiness? Do you look at yourself or others to exhibit the reality of those things or is your soul beholding the One who was the essential being of those things even before there was a man to attempt to be or demonstrate those things as mere attributes? At one time, peace for me was defined by the absence of contrary situations, but I have now seen it as from the beginning. For now peace has been and is being defined in my heart as the One who was peace even before there was an adverse situation in which to find myself.

Our glorious salvation has eternal context. So my prayer is that our souls begin and continue to know our salvation in this eternal context and experience fulfillment as from the beginning in the revealed presence of the Son of God.

CHAPTER FIVE

SALVATION –
A MATTER OF APPREHENSION

We have considered the external testimony that God gave concerning His Son. We have emphasized the fact that the elements to that testimony possessed an unseen, spiritual source. Because of this there was interwoven within their makeup a pregnant expectation concerning the coming of their Origin and Source. All of that is true, but the fact is that God did not need that testimony for Him to have in His view a full and perfect reality. He gave this testimony out from a full and perfect reality. Therefore, when I refer to fulfillment, I am not only referring to the fulfillment of the given testimony or even the fulfillment of types and figures; I am referring to the fulfillment of the purpose for our souls. You see, the types and the shadows were given by God as a testimony of the One for whom our souls exist. So fulfillment is the One who was eternally the view of the Father dwelling within the soul of the believer. I have written previously that fulfillment was never something that had to happen, but someone who had to come. God's concept of fulfillment was never an event but the coming of His Son as the Amen and Summation of every promise and prophecy concerning a full and perfect salvation.

Peter writes in 1 Peter 1:9-11, *"Receiving the end of your faith, even the salvation of your souls. Of which salvation the prophets have inquired and searched diligently, who prophesied of the grace that should come unto you: Searching what, or what manner of time the Spirit of Christ which was in them did signify, when it testified beforehand the sufferings of Christ, and the glory that should follow."* The salvation of which the prophets spoke and of which they inquired is the salvation we now have by grace and must now apprehend by faith. Notice this salvation is the salvation of the soul. The soul exists for this salvation.

How is it that we know and experience fulfillment as from the beginning? By fulfillment as from the beginning, I mean Christ in you. He is salvation and fulfillment as from the beginning. Not salvation and fulfillment as it has been defined by the ignorance of the natural mind, but as it has been eternally defined in the heart and perspective of the Father. It is that view and understanding the Father is well pleased to reveal in us.

Unfortunately, it seems that we are predisposed to think of the Beginning and the End linearly. We do that even when we read Jesus saying, **"I AM the Beginning and the End."** We need to look at it in the more comprehensive eternal viewpoint. God did not need a testimony. The testimony is given to us, but we cannot substitute the beauty of the testimony for the exceeding beauty and glory of the revealed Son of which is speaks. Your soul will never experience the Beginning and the End (the Fullness) of God's eternal thought and intention when attempting to know it with a linear mindset.

We know how perverted it has become when defined by times and events. Fulfillment, consummation and God's eternal intention cannot be known linearly it can only be realized in the face of the Person of the I AM Himself; because that is how God has defined it.

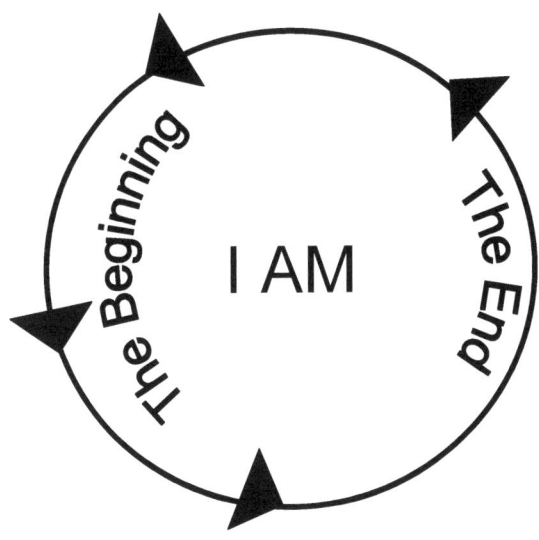

As the above diagram illustrates, the salvation we have in Christ can only be measured and defined in the eternalness of His Person. How can you comprehend the fullness promised of God if you are expecting that fullness in something that is divorced from His Person? It is not defined by something that is coming but who He is eternally.

When you read, "I AM the Alpha and the Omega," you will notice that the phrase, "the beginning and the end" is not actually found in the Greek manuscript. The thought and understanding of it is implied without a doubt. Alpha and Omega, as you know, is the first and the last letters of the Greek alphabet. This is a Greek usage, but the same thing was done in the Hebrew language. It was used by the Jews to describe the whole of a matter, the entirety of something. They used the **aleph** and the **tau,** which are the first letter and the last letter of the Hebrew alphabet. In the Hebrew, aleph and tau, when used together, speak of the summation of something. Jesus did not say that He was the aleph and then He would become the tau when His work was done. No! Notice where this declaration is being made; it is in the midst of His Church (the candlesticks). He declares Himself in the midst of His House and Body to be the whole of the matter. In the Spirit, on the Lord's Day, John beholds the One who is the embodiment of the whole and He sees Him living in the midst of His Church. Sadly, the majority of the Church has never seen the ALL OF ALL THINGS as a present indwelling reality. Christ did not need types and figures to become this. When He came, He came declaring Himself as who He had always been. He now lives within us. He is presently in the midst of His Church. Should our souls not be knowing Him as the whole and entirety of God's will and eternal intention? The Lord would have us to know a salvation far removed from situations, circumstances, and even external types and figures. He would reveal His view and eternal perspective in us. We should be in a constant state of realizing the eternal weight of salvation, the eternal weight of salvation is the Substance of Christ in us.

My point in this is that we are not a people who are awaiting fulfillment; we are not awaiting a coming consummation of all things. The fulfillment and consummation of all things presently dwells in us, the necessity that is upon us is growing up into Him, who is the Head in all things, growing in the grace and knowledge of the Lord Jesus Christ. It seems that we confuse the need of a coming consummation with the necessity of the inward comprehension of the consummation, who now resides within. For us, in Christ, salvation is a matter of knowledge. I do not mean an intellectual knowledge, but the knowledge of God being revealed in us. That is to say, that salvation is a matter of apprehension for us.

God has made available His eternal view to those of us who are in Christ. What a glorious thought! This view is the reason Paul can write in 2 Corinthians 3:7-11, *"But if the ministration of death, written and engraven in stones, was glorious, so that the children of Israel could not stedfastly behold the face of Moses for the glory of his countenance; which glory was to be done away: How shall not the ministration of the Spirit be rather glorious? For if the ministration of condemnation be glory, much more doth the ministration of righteousness exceed in glory. For even that which was made glorious had no glory in this respect, by reason of the glory that excelleth. For if that which is done away was glorious, much more that which remaineth is glorious."* The eternal and perfect glory is now in view. In comparison, the first is seen to be absolutely without glory at all. There was a prophesy of reality and now there is the reality present. In view of reality, the other is seen to be done away. It no longer remains, externally or internally.

We possess that which far exceeds types and shadows. We have the Son out from whom those elements proceeded. We have the very image of those things dwelling within. The One God receives and accepts, the One in whom and out from whom God did and said everything He ever did and said now lives in us. How much more can any person want, how much greater and more perfect can it get? It cannot be any greater than that. Then why are most still expecting more? Again, it is not a lack of completion, but a lack of soul comprehension. The problem is that most of us have not seen the greatness of Christ. We have not allowed God's perspective to be made apparent in our hearts, so we are still looking for fulfillment. Most are still looking for reality. Reality is continually present in your soul if you are born again. However, in whose face and in what creation are you seeking to find the reality of salvation?

The fact is, we have received and possess a perfect salvation, but most of us remain ignorant concerning its nature and makeup. Our salvation is Spirit and Truth. Once we remove it from the context of Spirit, we immediately make it void of Truth. In his book, *The New Life*, Andrew Murray writes, *"What hinders the believer with regard to the New Spiritual Life is chiefly ignorance of its nature, its Laws, and its workings. Man, even the Christian, has of himself not the least conception of the new life that comes from God: it surpasses all his thoughts. His own perverted thoughts of the way to serve and to please God, namely, by what he does and is, are so deeply rooted in him, that although he thinks that he understands and receives God's word, he yet thinks humanly and carnally on Divine things. Not only must God give salvation and life; He must also give the Spirit to make us know what He gives. Not only must He point out the land of Canaan, and the way thither; we must also, like the blind, be led every day by Himself. The Christian must try to cherish a deep conviction of his ignorance concerning the new life, and of his inability to form right thoughts about it."* This seems to be the dilemma for the believer. We are not aware of our incapacity with regard to the spiritual fullness to which we have come. We have come to a reality that is altogether new, a Life that is in no way familiar to us. However, because we do not understand, let alone cherish a deep conviction of our ignorance with regard to reality, we arrogantly attempt to perceive what is of God with the base faculties of the natural man. If we are to comprehend reality, and thereby cease being deceived and having our hearts diverted from Truth, then we must confess our ignorance and allow the Spirit of Truth to guide us where we have never gone before. The basis of our ignorance is a false sense of familiarity. By that I mean we bring into Christ our naturally derived and egocentric definitions, measurements and concepts with regard to spiritual reality. Therefore, we are thinking humanly upon spiritual things and most of us are oblivious to the difference.

This will be important and clearer as we proceed. Paul says in Galatians 2:6, *"the face of man God accepteth not."*[99] This beautifully defines the scope of the Father's sight. It is the same as saying that God does not look toward humanity in order to find what He desires. How many of us still do that, especially when it regards our own face? We are even told by some that if we do enough and are zealous enough, our face will even look like the face of Jesus. What a deceptive thing that is. It originates within the heart that still longs to look at self and find spiritual validity. However, God does not look at or receive the face of any man. We have been addressing that for the better part of this book. God's point of view has and will never change. There is One Face unto which He looks to define and measure His satisfaction and the fulfillment of His intention and it does not belong to any man. The glorious reality is that He desires to make that face the perspective of our hearts. The word "accepteth" means to look upon as to receive. It means first to look upon, but it means to look upon it as to receive something from it. Man's face is not the object upon which God looks to receive. The face unto which God presently looks is the face that has eternally been "in His eyes." In that one face, in that presence all fullness is found. He desires to reveal that face in us because the Light of the knowledge of the glory of God in the face of Jesus Christ alone will transform the soul from ignorance to His eternal understanding.[100] The question I

---

[99] Young's Literal Translation

[100] 2 Corinthians 4:6
For God who said, "Out of darkness let light shine," is He who has shone in our hearts to give us the light of the knowledge of God's glory, which is radiant on the face of Christ. – Weymouth

want to present to you is, "In whose face are you looking to observe the proof and evidence of spiritual reality (which is the only reality)?" I am speaking of the evidence of righteousness, holiness, glory, or perfection. In whose face and being do you suppose you will discover such evidence?

This takes us back to "I AM the Beginning and End." That is the same as Christ All and in All. That speaks of the "whole of the matter" now dwelling in the soul of His people. This may sound strange because of our linear view, but the Beginning is just as sufficient and perfect as the End. Christ being revealed by God in the realm of time and space, when God showed Him openly and sent Him to fulfill all of His pleasure,[101] did not cause Him to be more than who He was and is eternally. It permitted our souls to partake of the sufficiency of the Beginning and the End of God's eternal thought and of His finished work. In God's view, the Beginning was never awaiting the coming of the End. The Beginning was and is the End. In the Greek, actually, you can say it like this; I am the beginning, even the end. Christ in you is the comprehensive view of God the Father. Colossians 1:19, *"For it was the Father's gracious will that the whole of the divine perfections should dwell in Him."*[102] If you are born again, He has come to dwell in you and (as John writes) of His fullness have all we received. That has so much weight in my heart. It is amazing to think of how faithful our God is, how gracious God is to have given us the fullness of His eternally Beloved Son, the Son in whom His eternal pleasure and delight is manifest.

---

[101] Isaiah 55:11
So is My word that goeth out of My mouth, It turneth not back unto Me empty, But hath done that which I desired, And prosperously effected that [for] which I sent it. – Young's Literal Translation

[102] Weymouth New Testament

This book originated with one thought, Our salvation is God permitting our souls to partake of and participate in His own satisfaction through union with the Son who is His satisfaction. I have made emphasis upon those who hold to the vain concept of a fullness that is yet to come and are still waiting on God to finish His part of the deal as if He has yet to do so. Seeing those in this state breaks my heart. However, there is another group of people in the same state, just on a different side of that coin of ignorance. The people of whom I speak are those who totally believe and give mental assent to the fact that Christ is in them and that everything that they had at one time relegated to the future is now fulfilled in the Person of the indwelling Christ. They glory and confess with all confidence the fact that they possess in Christ all fullness, etc. To be honest I have been a part of both camps. They will say, "Those people preaching something to come are crazy, we have it all now." That sounds wonderful and it seems good, but the question that must be asked is has that reality actually become a subjective realization having effectual results in your heart? There is no doubt that you have all fullness in Christ, but is your soul actively apprehending that fullness, which you have received? You can try to stop believing a certain doctrine that you now realize to be false and attempt to believe a better doctrine, but if it is just doctrine and is the result of a natural mind attempting to intrude into spiritual fullness, it is no better than the previously held deception. They both attempt to define in the face of man what can only be defined in the Face of Christ. The revealing of Christ in the soul supersedes everything else and destroys it in the Light of His coming; it does not leave room for our thoughts, our doctrines, or our self-defined concepts. It leaves Him and that is it.

So what is the necessity that is upon us who have been given all fullness in Christ? There is the necessity of apprehending the fullness of Him. Now that does not mean to get something more than what you now have as a Christian. It does not mean to acquire or gather greater spiritual intelligence. I am speaking of the apprehending of which Paul speaks.

Philippians 3:12-13, *"Not as though I had already attained, either were already perfect: but I follow after, if that I may apprehend that for which also I am apprehended of Christ Jesus. Brethren, I count not myself to have apprehended: but this one thing I do, forgetting those things which are behind, and reaching forth unto those things which are before."* When Paul speaks of having not apprehended or of not having perfectly attained, he is not speaking objectively. He is speaking to the eternalness and unsearchableness of the fullness of Christ. With the vastness of Christ's fullness in view, Paul is not foolish enough to think that He has or shall ever exhaust the vastness of Christ's perfections. The knowing of Christ is an eternal journey that necessitates the guidance and unction of the Spirit of Truth within, taking of the fullness of Christ and showing that fullness to the soul He inhabits.[103] As we pursue in the Light, we will always be brought to the understanding that in all of our pursuing we have not even scratched the surface. We are still shallow, even upon the surface of the depths of Christ. It will never ever be exhausted. In the light of His dimensions, in the light of the depth of His person, you will always come to the realization, "I have not even scratched the surface of this reality." I remember reading something written by Brother T. Austin Sparks that so beautifully spoke to this. He wrote, *"We are always at the beginning of the knowing*

---

[103] John 16:15
All things that the Father hath are mine: therefore said I, that he shall take of mine, and shall shew it unto you.

of Christ." No matter how many years we have truly known Him, we are always just beginning. What a great and terrible thought. Recently the Lord spoke into my heart concerning this very thing. I was crying out to Him and asking Him if there would ever be a time in my life in Him where I would not feel as if I am scratching the surface. After several days of that, His voice resounded in me saying, *"No! You will never come to that time, because no matter how much of Me you have seen, there will never be less of Me to see."* Do you understand? The vastness of Christ our Life is far greater than the expanse of our ever-expanding natural universe. Why would that not be so, seeing that the natural universe proceeded out from the Son that lives within? That is important to understand because spiritual growth is the soul being awakened by God to all that He is in you. That is spiritual growth. That is what it means to apprehend. Spiritual apprehension is God revealing His Son in your heart, in ever-greater measure and we thereby experience an ever-greater realization of who it is that is in us and walk in the Light of that awareness.

In our pursuit of the knowing of Christ, we never apprehend anything greater than what we already have been given. That is impossible. We come to a God-given and Spirit-guided discovery of the greatness of the One who has been given. We are still speaking in terms of the Alpha and the Omega, the Eternal Word of whose fullness we have received. Therefore, in our pursuing of the knowledge of Him, in His eternalness, in His completeness, we never come to know anything greater than what has already been provided in our union with Him. In that God-given, soul-securing realization, we will cease looking for the greatness of salvation anywhere or in anyone else. We will say in Truth, "God, I know in me dwelleth no good thing, reveal in me your Son in whom all spiritual reality is measured and defined."

I want to consider salvation, which I have already defined above, as not a matter of completion as if it demands something that is lacking, but as a matter of apprehension. This is why the Apostle Paul says the Spirit of God has been given unto us. 1 Corinthians 2:12, *"Now we have received, not the Spirit of the world, but the Spirit which is of God; that we might know the things that are freely given to us of God."* That is why we have the Spirit of Truth, so that He may lead us and guide us into **the whole of the Truth.** We now have all of Truth because we have the Truth Himself within. However, the Spirit unveils our souls to the ALL TRUTH that He is. We have addressed the literal translation of Hebrews 6:1, *"Let us be carried along to that which is complete...."*[104] This literal rendering demonstrates the dependence of our souls upon the Spirit of Truth. It shows us that our progress and advancement in the knowing of the perfection of Christ is not a work we do, but is something that God does in us. It is performed by the power of another within us. How can you apprehend perfection? How can you proceed on to know the perfect and eternal fullness except the Spirit of God, whose fullness it is, makes it known in you? Only the Spirit of God knows the depths of God. The natural mind cannot know or apprehend it.[105] We must consider that reality, because

---

[104] The New Testament: An Expanded Translation by Kenneth S. Wuest Copyright © 1961 by Wm. B. Eerdmans Publishing Co.

[105] 1 Corinthians 2:11-14
For what man knoweth the things of a man, save the Spirit of man which is in him? even so the things of God knoweth no man, but the Spirit of God. Now we have received, not the Spirit of the world, but the Spirit which is of God; that we might know the things that are freely given to us of God. Which things also we speak, not in the words which man's wisdom teacheth, but which the Holy Ghost teacheth; comparing Spiritual

again, we are not dealing with a salvation that needs fulfillment, we are faced with fulfillment that demands the soul's apprehension. Salvation is a matter of apprehension, even apprehending what is already full and complete.

The reason so many Christians are dissatisfied and discontented with salvation is that there is a deficiency in their comprehension of salvation. If Christ, the Beloved of God, is not the One in our sight and the object of our heart's attention, we will see ourselves and suppose there to be a problem with salvation. The problem is our view. The problem is the face in which salvation has been defined for us. We look at ourselves and we see the falling short and we see the problems; we see us. That is a problem when attempting to know and apprehend spiritual reality. When we are the object of our own pursuits, and we believe that God's objective for us is self-betterment, self-improvement, or our spiritual enhancement, we are going to live disappointed, we are going to live unsatisfied every day of our lives. However, our God remains steadfast in His satisfaction because the view of His heart remains eternally fixed in the face of His Son.

Fortunately, the call of the Spirit in us is always come and see, come see the One I have seen from the beginning, come see the view of my heart. God's view has never deviated and He desires for our hearts to be unshakably fixed upon His Vision, the object of His satisfaction. He desires to reveal His Son in our souls.

What joy it is to have God's own eternal perspective revealed within. This is what Paul spoke of in Acts 26:19,

---

things with Spiritual. But the natural man receiveth not the things of the Spirit of God: for they are foolishness unto him: neither can he know them, because they are Spiritually discerned.

"Whereupon, O king Agrippa, I was not disobedient unto the heavenly vision." What constitutes this heavenly vision? Is this vision rapturous experiences or deep thoughts that come from heaven? Absolutely not! The Heavenly Vision is defined in this recounting of Paul's encounter with Christ. Acts 26:16, *"But rise, and stand upon thy feet, for for this I appeared to thee, to appoint thee an officer and a witness both of the things thou didst see, and of the things [in which] I will appear to thee."*[106] The Heavenly Vision is the perpetually effectual appearing of Christ, wherein all things of Life and Godliness are perfectly defined. This is not a one-time event but, as is said, "the things in which I will appear to thee." We do not have any idea what we now possess, and have no prayer of apprehending the fullness of it until Christ appears IN those things as their Very Image. Paul says that He was not disobedient to that vision. To be disobedient to the heavenly vision is to turn the gaze of our souls unto anything that is naturally observed and attempt to join that to what God alone reveals in the face of His vision. That is indeed what this heavenly vision is. It is the eternal vision of the Father of lights being revealed in us. That is the heavenly vision and it cannot be seen with natural eyes but must be revealed of God.

Instead of looking at ourselves in order to measure or exhibit reality, we must look into the countenance of Him who is reality and live there every moment of every day, walking in the Light of His countenance. However, this is not looking at Him and expecting that our faces will ever look like His. If that is the motivation, you have just deviated from Truth and Spirit, and God will never share His view with a heart that has such an egocentric motivation. The setting of the gaze of the soul upon the

---

[106] Young's Literal Translation

face of Jesus is unto the transforming and transitioning of the soul's comprehension from the glory that is no longer glorious to the exceeding glory of the indwelling Son of God; which is another way of saying until the soul is transformed into His same image. Do not be distracted; do not allow any vain philosophy of man to cause your heart to deviate from the simplicity of Christ.[107] Set you soul's intent and expectation unto His appearing, so in His appearing the vision of the Father can be made effectual in you. As I have already stated, the Father's view is eternally fixed, therefore He is not ignorant enough to look at us as to "accept our face." He does not lower His gaze. If that is so, should we not, as His people, have the same line of sight as our Father? The lack of that present vision is exactly why God can be eternally satisfied and we remain disenchanted, although we have been given all things in the Son. It is lack of vision, not visions, but the One God given heavenly vision. When that vision is ever before us, we can truly forget what is behind and pursue toward the apprehension of the vision ever before us. Paul writes in Philippians 3:13, *"But this one thing I do--forgetting everything which is past and stretching forward to what lies in front of me."*[108] What is he forgetting and putting behind him.[109] It does not refer

---

[107] Colossians 2:6-10
As ye have therefore received Christ Jesus the Lord, so walk ye in him: Rooted and built up in him, and stablished in the faith, as ye have been taught, abounding therein with thanksgiving. Beware lest any man spoil you through philosophy and vain deceit, after the tradition of men, after the rudiments of the world, and not after Christ. For in him dwelleth all the fulness of the Godhead bodily. And ye are complete in him, which is the head of all principality and power.

[108] Weymouth New Testament

[109] NT:1950 ἐπιλανθάνομαι epilanthanomai (ep-ee-lan-than'-om-ahee); middle voice from NT:1909 and NT:2990; to lose out of mind; by implication, to neglect: KJV - (be) forget (-ful of). *(Biblesoft's New Exhaustive Strong's Numbers and Concordance with Expanded Greek-Hebrew*

to bad things in his past or failures that he faced in times gone by. It refers to those very things he at one time counted as gain and of eternal worth. Forgetting what is behind is to have erased from the mind and heart that which is now behind the back. He has turned the gaze and affection of His heart upon the Father's own view and has thereby turned from his own self-centered view of Divine reality. It is the Father's Vision, the Eternal Son in whose face the Father finds His satisfaction, now fixed before the soul of Paul as the solitary object of His apprehension. That is why it must be with us as it was with Paul. It is never about acquiring something you do not have; it is apprehending the fullness in which you have begun. It has to become clear to us that, for us, it is all about apprehension. Apprehending the reality into which God, by His grace, has apprehended us.

When considering our apprehension of the fullness that God has provided in His Son, my mind goes directly to Joshua and the entrance into the land. This is very simple, but it makes a tremendous point for us who are in Christ. Joshua 1:1-3, *"Now after the death of Moses the servant of the Lord it came to pass, that the Lord spake unto Joshua the son of Nun, Moses' minister, saying, Moses my servant is dead; now therefore arise, go over this Jordan, thou, and all this people, unto the land which I do give to them, even to the children of Israel. Every place that the sole of your foot shall tread upon, that have I given unto you, as I said unto Moses." "After the death of Moses...."* I have already made the point that when you read the terms after or

---

Dictionary. Copyright © 1994, 2003, 2006 Biblesoft, Inc. and International Bible Translators, Inc.)

NT:3694 ὀπίσω a: a position behind an object or other position - 'behind, in back of. *(from Greek-English Lexicon Based on Semantic Domain. Copyright © 1988 United Bible Societies, New York. Used by permission.)*

afterwards, it speaks of a transition from the first order and administration of things to the Second administration of the fullness of Christ in a people. The journey we are going to consider must be seen in the Light of God's eternal perspective.

Notice this, *"I do give to them even the children of Israel...that have I given you as I said unto Moses."* Also in Joshua 1:6, *"Be strong and of a good courage: for unto this people shalt thou divide for an inheritance the land, which I sware unto their fathers to give them."* After this transition from Moses to Joshua, we are immediately faced with the fulfillment of the promise God made to Moses and the fathers of Israel. God made a promise and now He is giving them the reality that He promised. Can you see the perfect connection with the following verses? Acts 13:32-33, *"And we declare unto you glad tidings, how that the promise which was made unto the fathers, God hath fulfilled the same unto us their children, in that he hath raised up Jesus again; as it is also written in the second psalm, Thou art my Son, this day have I begotten thee."* Hebrews 1:1-2, *"God, who at sundry times and in divers manners spake in time past unto the fathers by the prophets, Hath in these last days spoken unto us by his Son, whom he hath appointed heir of all things, by whom also he made the worlds."* In Christ, we are immediately faced with the fulfillment of all promises and prophecies made of God unto the fathers.

Now, that is absolute, it is reality for us in Christ. We have been brought into the fullness and fulfillment of the whole of what God promised. However, that brings upon us a great necessity: apprehension. Joshua 1:2-3, *"...Unto the land which I do give to them, even to the children of Israel. Every place that **the sole of your foot shall tread upon**, that have I given unto you, as I said unto Moses."* What God has given demands that we tread upon it. Notice, *"Every* *place the sole of your foot shall tread upon, have I given it to you."* We think apprehending salvation has to do with gathering what we do not have, but it is not according to this. Every place you tread upon, every place you walk, **I have** already given. What you must do is apprehend what I have already given. I love that. This is what I mean by salvation is a matter of apprehension. God has already given us all things that pertain unto life and godliness.[110] Ephesians 2:8-9, *"For by grace are ye saved through faith; and that not of yourselves: it is the gift of God: Not of works, lest any man should boast."* The gift has been given. So what now? Walk. Colossians 2:6, *"As ye have therefore received Christ Jesus the Lord, so walk ye in him."* Galatians 5:25, *"If we live in the Spirit, let us also walk in the Spirit."* God is calling unto the soul, "Apprehend the ground and the land unto which I have brought you." We understand that the length, breadth, and depth of this good land is measured by the eternal dimensions of Christ. God is calling us to allow the Spirit of Truth to guide us into the fullness He has given.

In the Hebrew language, the phrase "have I given" is in the perfect tense, which means that when God says this, He is speaking from a point of completion, as an already completed situation.[111] God is speaking in view of a

---

[110] 2 Peter 1:2-4
Grace and peace be multiplied unto you through the knowledge of God, and of Jesus our Lord, According as his divine power hath given unto us all things that pertain unto life and godliness, through the knowledge of him that hath called us to glory and virtue: Whereby are given unto us exceeding great and precious promises: that by these ye might be partakers of the divine nature, having escaped the corruption that is in the world through lust.

[111] HEBREW PERFECT - Earlier grammars characterized the suffix conjugation as indicating completed action; however, it is better to view it as indicating a "complete situation." "The perfect serves to express

fulfilled condition. I have given it freely to you, now you must apprehend the fullness of the gift. John says, "Of His fullness have all we received," so what does that leave for us? It leaves **before us** the apprehension of the fullness that He is.

God is saying this to the Second Israel. He is presenting them with fulfillment and saying, *"Lift up now thine eyes from whence thou art...walk through the land in the length of it and in the breadth of it."*[112] They are to walk in the fulfillment of the promise given by God unto Moses. They are to walk in the realization of what He spoke unto Moses and the promise He made unto the fathers. Does this not sound familiar? Acts 26:22, *"Having therefore obtained help of God, I continue unto this day, witnessing both to small and great, saying none other things than those which the prophets and Moses did say should come."* Paul came declaring this very reality. He declared to the Church that God had fulfilled all things promised unto the fathers in the risen Christ and that the fullness of Christ was for our apprehending. God is calling us to experience something that is already happening, already given, already taking place. Let me emphasize again that our pursuit is not about getting something that is lacking but inwardly possessing the reality in which God has already made us to stand.

Romans 5:2, *"By whom also we have access by faith into this grace wherein we stand, and rejoice in hope of the glory of God."* We already stand **in** the grace of God; we already stand in the all sufficiency of Christ. It is in grace

---

actions, events, or states, which the speaker wishes to represent from the point of view of completion...[and]..are pictured as in their completed state." *(from Wheeler's Hebrew Syntax Notes, Copyright © 1988-2006 by Rev. Prof. Dale M. Wheeler, Ph.D. All rights reserved. Used by permission.)*

[112] Genesis 13:14-17

that Christ is made unto us righteousness, redemption, sanctification, all spiritual blessings. That is our present state of being. However, it is exclusively by faith that we possess that grace in which we presently stand. Faith is the beholding of Christ; the seeing of Him as the embodiment of all spiritual substance. It is in that God-given view or vision that we possess in Truth what God has already given. Instead of constantly attempting to acquire a ground that we assume still eludes us, it is faith by which we apprehend the heavenly ground upon which we already stand. Faith does not guide us upon any other ground. We attempt to bring faith into the earth and have it function there, but faith is the faculty that beholds the unseen perfections of the indwelling Christ, the eternal proportions of His substance.

So how is it that we apprehend the good land that God has given? Joshua 3:2-3, *"And it came to pass after three days, that the officers went through the host; And they commanded the people, saying, When ye see the ark of the covenant of the Lord your God, and the priests the Levites bearing it, then ye shall remove from your place, and go after it."* First, notice that this was a command given to the people. This was not a suggestion half-heartedly passed about the people, but a command of God conveyed to them. If they were to apprehend and possess this land that God had given, they must obey this command. What is the command? *"When you see the ark of the covenant of the Lord your God...."* The first aspect of this command is SEEING THE ARK. How will you possess this land? You must first SEE THE ARK.

When we talk about the ark, it should bring us back to the point we have been making previously in these pages. What does the ark of the Covenant represent? The ark is God's exclusive perspective, only God saw it. No man could see it. It was veiled; no man could look upon it. No man could touch it or see it. It was God's viewpoint. The beginning of the journey of apprehension is SEEING God's own perspective. The beginning of our walk is God revealing and bringing before our soul's eye the exclusive viewpoint of the Father, the simplicity and singleness of Christ being openly shown to the soul.

Another aspect of this command is, *"When ye see the ark of the covenant of the Lord your God, and the priests the Levites bearing it, then* **ye shall remove from your place, and go after it**.*"* I cannot fail to mention the fact that the priests were bearing this object of God's perspective. It is very dangerous to follow those that are not bearing this heavenly vision, for you will be led astray. I will leave that. The result of seeing the ark is, *"Ye shall remove yourself from your place and go after it."* I hope the significance of this statement grabs you, but you cannot and will never leave YOUR place until you first SEE THE ARK. I have seen many people leave doctrines and concepts behind for what they deem to be better ones, but it is nothing more than another familiar place. They never left their place, they just thought they improved their place, but the place where they went was still defined and measured by their own understanding and measurements. I remember a time when I began hearing teachings concerning how the common belief of Christ's second coming was not accurate. Due to the convincing nature of their argument, I made up my mind that I was no longer going to believe in that scripturally inaccurate concept. I started believing what I deemed to be a better teaching. The problem was that even though I had what I believed to be a better doctrine, I actually still had nothing more than another doctrine of which I was convinced. Honestly, I was just as confused as ever. Although I had a new strong belief, I had not seen the ark, and until I saw the ark or until Christ appeared **in that thing**, I could not leave MY PLACE. Even my new concept of the second coming was self-centered and self-defined. What I am trying to convey is that until you see the ark (have Christ revealed in your soul), you can and will hold to a better and even accurate teaching but still never experience the reality of that certain aspect of salvation. Until I experienced the coming of the Lord in my heart in the appearing of Christ, I could not leave a concept of salvation that had me as its center. It is impossible. God must reveal His Son as the reality of every aspect of salvation or we cannot know. When that takes place, it is no longer an issue of leaving something, but one of pursuing the ark that God has set before the eyes of the soul. It becomes a matter of pursuing the greater reality, not giving up a lesser. It is about following on to know Him who is real and perfect. That is the only means of apprehending the fullness of our Great Salvation: pursuing in sight of the ark. You leave your place only when your soul is going after God's view. Do you remember Philippians 3? Forgetting what is behind (your place) and pursuing that which is set out before the soul as the object of eternal pursuit (the ark).

The next verse is very significant to my argument in this chapter. Joshua 3:4, *"Yet there shall be a space between you and it, about two thousand cubits by measure: come not near unto it, that ye may know the way by which ye must go: for ye have not passed this way heretofore."* Come not near unto it. Now that just stood out to me a few weeks ago. I am convinced that this statement perfectly encompasses the problem with most Christians and is the reason why most are hindered on their journey in Christ. As those who desire to possess and know the Lord and apprehend His fullness, we cannot make the mistake of bringing the ark near unto us.

We can all understand the desire to apprehend the vast and glorious land that is set before us in Christ, but to do this the command is, *'Set the ark out a large space from yourself and come not near unto it.'* That still appears to me to be the real root of the problem for most Christians. This may sound strange to the mind of man, but the reality of our salvation must always be defined separate from us. I understand that may sound strange and you would ask, but what about union with Christ. When I speak of reality being defined and measured as to its separateness from us, I do not mean separate as to union, but as to its meaning, identity, and substance. The ark was always in their midst. However, when it came to their apprehension of the land given, it had to be SEEN TO BE AT A SPACE FROM THEM AND NOT BROUGHT NEAR. In order to possess the fullness of the Promise of God, it had to be done in sight of something that was far removed from them.

There was a warning concerning bringing it too close. Joshua 3:4, *"...come not near unto it, that ye may know the way."* If they brought the ark too close to themselves, they would not know the way. How true that is. How many Christians today love the Lord and want to know Him, but the problem is that they are attempting to bring what God beholds in the face of His Son, too close to themselves and attempting to define it with themselves in view. Righteousness, holiness, perfection, love, peace, sanctification; what damage has been done to the hearts of sincere Christians because these terms that are defined in the nature and Life of Christ have been brought into the earth and falsely defined in the face of natural men. No wonder so many are lost and do not know the way. Our souls must be unveiled to God's eternal vision or we will continually attempt to find the evidence of spiritual reality with flesh and blood in view. The Eternal Vision of the Father was fixed on the face of the Son before ever a man was created, so how can man ever be the object of His perspective. It is that vision that must be revealed within us.

An attempt to define what is spiritual in view of that which is natural, has caused so many well-meaning hearts to be deceived. That is why God must reveal His Son and thereby define the scope of our soul's pursuit. This journey is one of absolute dependence on our part. Why? *"...For ye have not passed this way heretofore."* This is not a way or a land that is familiar to you at all and it cannot be known or possessed when you attempt to do so in view of what is familiar. The seeing and following after the ark will never take us onto familiar ground. Newness of Life is unrecognizable to our own understanding, until newness is defined properly in the face of the correct man.

It is important to understand that spiritual reality must always be comprehended in its separateness from us as to its identity, its measure, and its substance. Salvation must finally be defined inwardly in the "otherness of Christ." In other words, the evidence and measurement of any aspect of salvation must be realized in view of "not I, but Christ" who lives within the soul. Our apprehension of the Land given of God must be in view of the object of God's own perspective; a perspective that is far removed from ourselves.

I am speaking of continually walking and pursuing in the Light of the salvation that is without sin. That is what the Hebrew writer declares. Christ appears as the Second, without sin, as our full and perfect salvation. But He appears to those who look for Him, not to those who are looking at themselves in order to find the proof of the reality that is exclusively found in the revealed presence of Christ. All things must be known, measured, and apprehended as who He is, not as what we become. Again, the question should be asked, "In whose face are we seeking to behold spiritual substance?" Has righteousness become familiar to us? Has love become familiar to us? In other words, is the evidence of these spiritual realities still sought in the familiarity of self, or do we continually approach our salvation with the knowledge of our dependence upon the Spirit of Truth to guide us into the Truth of a reality that we can never know on our own. Left to our own devices, we will without fail attempt to put a human face on divine perfection.

Philippians 3:9, *"And be found in him, not having mine own righteousness, which is of the Law, but that which is through the faith of Christ, the righteousness which is of God by faith."* As one actively beholding the Lord, seeing the Ark, Paul says, *"To be found in Him not having mine own righteousness."* Paul is seeing the righteousness as it is defined in the eyes of the Father, and now it is by faith that he is apprehending the righteousness he at one time believed himself to possess by observance of Law. However, that supposed righteousness was defined TO CLOSE to himself. Now Paul is beholding the Essential Being of righteousness that stood as God's perspective before there was a man to ever attempt to call himself righteous. That is how every spiritual term must finally come to be defined in our hearts; it must be defined according to its eternal context, or better said, in view of its eternal source and meaning. We do not truly begin to progress in this journey of apprehension until the revealed Christ becomes the perspective in which we are walking. Until He is the object before us we are going to attempt to get God to add to us and to define, by us, the things that belong exclusively to Christ.

If we go to 2 Peter we will see the necessity of salvation being seen and comprehended as separate from ourselves. 2 Peter 1:9, *"But he that lacketh these things is blind, and cannot see afar off."* It is important to realize that Peter is addressing those who have been made partakers of the

Divine Nature, therefore due to that being their state of being, there is nothing of fullness lacking, in fact it has been fully supplied in union with Christ. However, Peter is addressing those in whom the reality seems to be "non present". The problem in this scenario is not actual absence of spiritual reality, but attempting to know that reality in view of the wrong man. He writes of those to whom these things are not present. He does not mean that they are actually lacking, but the believer is ignorant of the presence of spiritual fullness. What causes such ignorance? It is blindness. Yet, we must examine Peter's definition of blindness. Is it total lack of vision? No! It is the lack of God's vision. The problem, as stated, is self-assessment. Man attempting to find reality when looking at himself. That is what he means by, *"he is blind and cannot see afar off."* The English Standard Version translates it, *"he is so nearsighted that he is blind."* Nearsighted is a good way of saying it, but what does it actually mean? This is very critical when seeing the necessity of seeing salvation defined "afar off" from ourselves.

The Greek term for the English phrase "cannot see afar off" actually means the inability to observe anything that is not NEAR.[113] It also brings in the appearance, the countenance. Therefore, the blindness that causes the presence of spiritual fullness to seem to be lacking is actually the inability to behold a reality that is not defined with man's own face in view. This blind man cannot see the evidence of a reality that is removed from his own countenance. Such

---

[113] NT:3467 muopazo (μυωπάζω, NT:3467), "to be short-sighted" (muo, "to shut," ops, "the eye"; cf. Eng., "myopy," "myopic": the root mu signifies a sound made with closed lips, e. g., in the words "mutter," "mute"), occurs in 2 Peter 1:9, RV, **"seeing only what is near"** (KJV, "and cannot see afar off"); **this does not contradict the preceding word "blind," it qualifies it**. *(Vine's Expository Dictionary of Biblical Words, Copyright © 1985, Thomas Nelson Publishers.)*

blindness stops the soul's apprehension of Christ. How many of us are presently attempting to define the Divine Nature by looking at us? BLIND! Blindness is looking at self and sight is seeing Christ. We cannot apprehend the length and breadth of Him when we are blind. *Vincent Word Studies* gives another view of this word by writing, "the participle 'being short-sighted' is added to the adjective 'blind,' **defining it**; as if he had said, 'is blind,' **that is**, 'short-sighted' spiritually; seeing only things present and not heavenly things."[114] Seeing things present is seeing things that are readily available to the natural faculties and attempting to define the Diving Nature accordingly. However, such a false view causes the soul to neglect and count as absent what is heavenly or what is exclusively known and made known of God. We must see the Ark that God has set "afar off" from us.

To end this chapter, I want to share a portion of a wonderful book by T. Austin Sparks entitled *School of Christ*. This is a portion from the second chapter of that book; the heading is *Living By the Truth*. What we have been occupied with in this chapter can be encapsulated in that phrase. Seeing the Ark afar off from us is walking and living in and by The Truth. To apprehend the salvation given of God, you cannot ever define it with yourself in view. That is the point being made by Brother Sparks. Where is Truth defined? He writes, *"Will you accept it from me when I say that there is no truth in us. In us by nature there is no truth. I am going to get right down inside this thing, What is a Christian? A Christian is one who was not a very good tempered person but is now a good tempered person. He was not a very genial person but is now much more genial. He was a*

---

[114] Vincent's Word Studies in the New Testament, Electronic Database. Copyright © 1997, 2003, 2005, 2006 by Biblesoft, Inc. All rights reserved.

person not very zealous or active but is now very zealous, a person who is different in disposition from what he was formerly. Is that a true definition of a Christian? Give me a homeopathic cabinet. Bring along to me a very irritable person and give him a dose of a medication that deals with emotional problems. In two or three hours, he will be a very good tempered man. Is he a Christian now? Give him something else; turn him back into what he was before. Was he saved before? Has he backslidden? Drugs can be used to change a man's temper in a few hours. From being lethargic, careless, and indifferent, he becomes alive, energetic, and active. From being miserable and discontented, morose, melancholic and disagreeable, he becomes amiable, pleasant, and relieved from all the nervous strain, which was making him like that; all that disordered digestion, which was making him such a bore to live with. For a little while, you have made a Christian with drugs. You see the point. Where is the truth? Where is the truth? If the truth about my salvation lies in the realm of feelings, my digestive system, my nervous organism, I'm going to be a poor Christian because that will be changing from day to day according to whether or not something else changes. Oh no, where is the truth found? Not what I am but what Thou art. That is the truth. You shall know that truth and the truth shall make you free. Free from what? Bondage. But what bondage? Satan clapping his chains of condemnation upon you because today you're not feeling up to scratch. You are feeling bad in your constitution and you are feeling depressed. You are feeling death all around you, you feel irritable and Satan comes along and says you're not a Christian. Fine Christian you are, and you go down under that. Is that the truth? The only answer for deliverance and emancipation is it is not who I am it is who Christ is. Christ abides the same...." Friend, contrary to us, there is no variableness in Him. That is the Truth. That is reality. That fixed reality is God's eternal perspective. Our self-measured concepts of right standing with God can be altered from day to day depending on a multitude of things, but Christ remains the same. He is not as we are. Let us allow God to reveal reality far removed from ourselves and come not near it.

Brother Sparks continues, *"...He is other than we are, varying here in this human life from hour to hour, day to day, He is other. What is the truth? It is that which delivers us from this false self that we are...."* How deceived must we be to look at our false self in order to attempt to define Truth? It is the coming of the Truth, the seeing of the Ark that delivers us from the false self we are. *"...What is the truth? It is that which delivers us from this false self that we are and we are a false self. We are a bundle of contradictions We can never be sure if we are going to be of the same mind for long or that our convictions are not going to do a right about turn. No, truth is not ourselves at all. It is Christ."* That is what I have been attempting to say. If you bring it too close, you cannot know the way, if you bring it too close you will not apprehend what God has given, you will substitute yourself for it and remain blind and in your familiar place. Let us turn our hearts, for it is the pleasure of God to make known and cause us to apprehend our Great Salvation in its eternal context.

CHAPTER SIX

COMPARING SPIRITUAL THINGS WITH SPIRITUAL

We are concerned with the soul's apprehension of the gift of grace, which has permitted us to partake of God's own eternal satisfaction. In the previous chapter, we looked at Joshua chapter 1 where the Lord spoke to Israel concerning the Land that He had given them. How very significant it is that in the Hebrew text this phrase, "have I given," is in the perfect tense, which means that God is speaking to them out from and in view of an already fulfilled condition. The land was not progressively given of God, but given of God as a whole to His people. Unfortunately, most of us falsely believe that what God provides us in Christ, is progressively given, but that is not the case. It is our comprehension of what God has given that is progressive. It is the progressive work of the Spirit. What God has given is full, complete, and perfect, because what He has given is nothing short of the fullness and perfection of His Son. He has not given us His Son in pieces and parts. He testified of His Son in pieces and parts,[115] but when He gives His Son to the soul created for Him, He does not give that Son in

---

[115] Hebrews 1:1-2

pieces and parts; *"of His fullness, have all we received."*[116] I remember hearing for many years something along the lines of, "we have a small Jesus now, but He gets bigger in us as we faithfully perform all the prescribed religious observances." Jesus does not get bigger in us, nor do we get more of Jesus as we go. Our comprehension of His greatness grows if we will permit the Spirit of Truth to guide us into the depths of His full measure.

In Joshua, God tells Israel, *"Every place that your foot shall tread upon I have given it."* He does not say when you tread upon it, I will give it to you. He tells them, "What you tread upon is that which I have already given." They did not have to wait on the land to be given, the necessity was apprehending what God had given, which was the fulfillment of the promise God made to Moses and the Fathers. Therefore, it becomes evident that for us in Christ, salvation is not a matter of obtaining something we have imagined to be absent, but it is a matter of laying hold of and discovering the vastness of what God has given in and as His Son. It is not a work on our part; it is our souls submitting to the work of the Spirit; the work only He can do, for He makes known depths that only He knows. Yet, there has to be a heart willing to submit to that work of God.

Then we looked at the means of this apprehension. Joshua 3:3-4, *"And they commanded the people, saying, When ye see the ark of the covenant of the Lord your God, and the priests the Levites bearing it, then ye shall remove from your place, and go after it. Yet there shall be a space between you and it, about two thousand cubits by measure: come not near unto it, that ye may know the way by which ye must go: for ye have not passed this way heretofore."*

---

[116] John 1:16

They could not merely send a memo throughout the camp and let them know that the ark was somewhere up the road. They had to see the ark themselves in order for the object of pursuit to actually be defined in their own sight. That is the same with us. It is said to them that they could never know the way except they see the ark that is set afar off from them. If we bring the ark too near, all we will do is walk within the darkness of our own vain imaginations and in that state, we are constantly tripping over our own illusions. The Spirit guides us in the Truth by always keeping the ark (Christ the exclusive perspective of the Father) ever before the eyes of the soul. He does not have a rope pulling us by the neck. He has an object that He places before the eyes of the soul and says **go after it**; **pursue**. God does not tell you to pursue things or natural situations. The Son is the sole object God sets before us for our pursuit. Colossians 3:1, *"If, then, ye were raised with the Christ, the things above seek ye...."*[117] Set your affection within the confines of where you are and do not allow your soul's attention and affection to be deviated. Do not look to the right or to the left. The orientation of your heart must be upon the ark or else you will never know or apprehend the *"riches of the glory of his inheritance in the saints"*[118] and *"the exceeding riches of His grace in His kindness toward us through Christ Jesus."*[119]

In the beginning of this book, I referred to Genesis 1:31, *"And God saw every thing that he had made, and, behold, it was very good."* God saw everything that He had made. He did not look at certain aspects of it. He saw it all. This is God's view. God beholds the WHOLE OF THE

---

[117] Young's Literal Translation

[118] Ephesians 1:18

[119] Ephesians 2:7

MATTER. Remember that the whole of the matter is expressed in the declaration, "I AM the Beginning and the End." He sees everything of His work perfectly summed up in One Glorious Son. That is God's view. We understand that God used multitudes of things and multitudes of people. God created men and places and cities, etc. He did it all in view of and as a testimony of One eternal substance. Proverbs 8:15-16, *"By me kings reign, and princes decree justice. By me princes rule, and nobles, even all the judges of the earth."* They were set up and cast down; and in the raising up of kings and the casting down of kings, people, and nations, He was giving testimony of His Son. Those people and places were never meant to be something unto themselves, they were used of God as a testimony of the Truth; the meaning for which they existed came in the coming of the Son. So why did He do all of this? It was so that we would have a testimony unto which we could go and be able to say, "This is what we have come to." So many are intrigued with the glory of the testimony, but the testimony was and continues to be UNTO the appearing of the exceeding glory of the Person of whom it spoke. You cannot see the embodiment and reality of what you have come to, except you behold it in the face of Jesus Christ. However, the testimony is essential as well; it must be there, but the Truth must appear in us that we may see God's full intention for the testimony. Jesus came to "confirm the covenant."[120] He came as the affirmation and surety of the first covenant. He did not disregard the testimony of that age, but said, *"Do not for a moment suppose that I have come to abrogate the Law or*

---

[120] Daniel 9:27
And he shall confirm the covenant with many for one week: and in the midst of the week he shall cause the sacrifice and the oblation to cease, and for the overspreading of abominations he shall make it desolate, even until the consummation, and that determined shall be poured upon the desolate.

the Prophets: I have not come to abrogate them but to give them their completion."[121] He utilized the testimony in order to show Himself as its completion. *"I Am the Door," "I Am the Bread which came down from heaven," "Your father Abraham rejoiced to see my day: and he saw it, and was glad," "Jesus said unto them, Verily, verily, I say unto you, Before Abraham was, I Am," "Behold, a greater than Solomon is here.", "But I say unto you, That in this place is one greater than the temple," "Jesus said unto her, I am the resurrection, and the life: he that believeth in me, though he were dead, yet shall he live."*[122] This is just to name a few. He brings them back to the testimony; however, He does not leave them within the empty shadows of that testimony. He is bringing them unto Himself as the testimonies fulfillment. He is not the destruction of it but the revealed intention of it.

The writer of Hebrews sets forth at the onset of the letter that the prophecies and testimony were actually given of God, but that they were unto the coming of an end and goal. The intention of this letter was to attempt to bring them from those shadows to the substance Himself. He begins it with God as the origin of the testimony and then the Son as the conclusion of it. Paul (who I believe wrote Hebrews) never destroyed the Law, he never nullified God as its source, as if it had no purpose for existing. He is saying, "God did give this beautiful testimony to you, but He did not intend for you to stay forever within it, He did it to testify of the One who now lives in you, so now let us submit our hearts that the Spirit would guide us on into His own eternal perfection." The necessity of the guidance of

---

[121] Matthew 5:17 – Weymouth New Testament

[122] John 10:9, John 6:41, John 8:56, John 8:58, Matthew 12:42, Matthew 12:6, John 11:25

the Spirit is in order that we would behold the perfection of the indwelling Christ and apprehend the glories of His fullness. That cannot be done with self in view. That cannot be done with types and shadows in view. You cannot apprehend the fullness of His reality when you are still looking at a nation across the ocean and believing that nation to be the Israel of God. We must at least scripturally agree with the fact that Paul did not even look at the Church, as a collection of people, and say that it is the Israel of God. He looked at Christ and declared the Son to be the Israel of God; the only Prince with God. He is the substance of Israel's testimony. The glory of it is that He lives in us. There is a school of theological thought known as Preterism. One strong theological belief of this group is that the Church has replaced Israel in the heart and mind of God. I was recently asked if I believed in this concept known as "replacement theology." I told them that I did not believe in replacement theology, but in "fulfillment theology." God did not replace a group of people with another group of people; He fulfilled the testimony that was set forth in a people in the coming of the Person of fulfillment.

We begin in a state of fulfillment in Christ, and the Spirit of God works upon that premise. There is nothing unfulfilled and imperfect in Christ besides our understanding, and the Spirit's work is to reveal His understanding of Christ's fullness in our hearts. The Spirit of God exclusively works in our hearts in view of what God declares to be "very good". He does this in order that we may know the 'very good' into which we have been brought. That is what Paul desired for the Church to which He ministered. Colossians 2:1-3, *"I want you to know how great a struggle I have on your behalf and for those who are at Laodicea, and for all those who have not personally seen my face, that their hearts may be encouraged, having been knit together in love, and attaining to all the wealth that comes from the full assurance of understanding, resulting in a true knowledge of God's mystery, that is, Christ Himself. in whom are hidden all the treasures of wisdom and knowledge."*[123] The full knowledge of God's mystery, who is Christ. Paul is speaking of his desire that the Lord's Body come to behold in fullness the eternal substance that was hidden, as a mystery, under the Old Covenant system. The vastness of the riches that are in Christ were described by Paul as "unsearchable and past finding out".[124] It is past finding out with the human mind, it is unknowable to the human intellect, and unsearchable to the natural mind. Unsearchable does not mean that you cannot find it and it cannot be known. Unsearchable means you are not the one that can find it or make it known. We have the unsearchable riches set before us in Christ and only the Spirit of God can make Him known.

1 Corinthians 2:9-14. *"But as it is written, Eye hath not seen, nor ear heard, neither have entered into the heart of man, the things which God hath prepared for them that love him. But God hath revealed them unto us by his Spirit: for the Spirit searcheth all things, yea, the deep things of God. For what man knoweth the things of a man, save the Spirit of man which is in him? even so the things of God knoweth no man, but the Spirit of God. Now we have received, not the Spirit of the world, but the Spirit which is of God; that we might know the things that are freely given to us of God. Which things also we speak, not in the words which man's wisdom teacheth, but which the Holy Ghost teacheth;*

---

[123] New American Standard

[124] Romans 11:33-34
O the depth of the riches both of the wisdom and knowledge of God! how unsearchable are his judgments, and his ways past finding out! For who hath known the mind of the Lord? or who hath been his counsellor?

comparing spiritual things with Spiritual. But the natural man receiveth not the things of the Spirit of God: for they are foolishness unto him: neither can he know them, because they are Spiritually discerned." I want to concentrate on a portion of these verses, which is not discussed very often. However, to me it is one of the most significant parts of this portion of scripture.

Here Paul is addressing the "hidden wisdom," the wisdom of God that was hidden in times past, but was made known and fully displayed in the Cross of Christ. 1 Corinthians 2:6-8, *"Howbeit we speak wisdom among them that are perfect: yet not the wisdom of this world, nor of the princes of this world, that come to nought: But we speak the wisdom of God in a mystery, even the hidden wisdom, which God ordained before the world unto our glory: Which none of the princes of this world knew: for had they known it, they would not have crucified the Lord of glory."* In reference to this he now writes, *"But as it is written, Eye hath not seen, nor ear heard, neither have entered into the heart of man, the things which God hath prepared for them that love him."*

Although this portion has been misunderstood as a statement, regarding a future fulfillment, where we will see made manifest what we cannot now see, in the context of the verses, it is obviously concerning the reality that has been provided and secured in and by Christ and Him Crucified. The phrase "hath not seen" is made up of two Greek words. "Not" is the word ου ou (oo) which is the absolute negative meaning never or not at all.[125] The phrase "hath seen" is the Greek word εἴδω eido which means to

---

[125] NT:3756 ου ou (oo)
(Biblesoft's New Exhaustive Strong's Numbers and Concordance with Expanded Greek-Hebrew Dictionary. Copyright © 1994, 2003, 2006 Biblesoft, Inc. and International Bible Translators, Inc.)

possess knowledge by seeing.[126] It also has the meaning, *"to comprehend the meaning of something, with focus upon the resulting knowledge."*[127] This phrase is also in the aorist active tense. That tells us that it is not just speaking of lack of perception in the past, but the perpetual incapacity of the natural faculties in relation to the spiritual meaning of what God has fully provided in Christ. There are things that the eyes did and could see and the ears did and could hear. There were things that were readily accessible to the natural mind, but the spiritual meaning of them could not be observed.

In reference to this, I share another article written by Brother Sparks. He writes, *"The coming of Christ stands as the dividing of two whole systems. And we must consider the essential nature of this great divide. The obvious nature of the old Jewish dispensation was that it was all in the realm of the natural senses. It was in the realm of physical senses. Everything was a matter of seeing with the physical eye, of hearing with the physical ear, of feeling with the physical hand. It was something that could be touched, something that was tangible. Their whole system rests upon the physical senses. God gave them a tabernacle that they could see and handle; God gave them the incense that they could smell; God gave them the feasts that they could taste; however, they were blind to the meaning of these things. What is the essential nature of that which has come in with Jesus Christ? It is a spiritual order."* This is essential to see. The natural faculties could perceive the natural order of a natural testimony. However, the meaning of it was actually never observed, nor could it ever be. Because when

---

[126] NT: 1492 εἴδω (eido)

[127] Greek-English Lexicon Based on Semantic Domain. Copyright © 1988 United Bible Societies, New York. Used by permission.

confronted with the eternal vastness of the Son, it is evident how insufficient our observational faculties truly are. Again, this is Paul's point in these verses. He desires to expose the impotence of man's understanding in view of the eternal depths of Christ and thereby expose our dependence upon the Spirit of God to know anything that has been prepared or made ready by God in Christ. This lack of capacity with regard to reality is the wellspring of all self-delusion.

I must not get caught here, so I will move on. 1 Corinthians 2:9, *"Eye hath not seen, nor ear heard, neither have entered into the heart of man, the things which God hath prepared for them that love him."* This incapacity in perception is not with regard to future things at all as some would suggest. It is in relation to what God hath prepared. The phrase "hath prepared" is the same phrase that we encounter in Matthew 22:2-4, when we see the King who prepared a dinner for His Son. The wonderful declaration made, *"Behold, I have prepared my dinner: my oxen and my fatlings are killed, and all things are ready: come unto the marriage."* It does not take much study to realize that what God has prepared and this marriage dinner that is prepared by the Father (oxen and fatlings) is without a doubt speaking of what the Cross has fulfilled and made ready for those who will come and partake. Paul is stressing the fact that no man can know or partake of this feast God has made ready and provided for us in Christ, when attempting to do it with his own understanding.

Paul is actually partially quoting from the Prophet Isaiah in these verses. Isaiah 64:4, *"For since the beginning of the world men have not heard, nor perceived by the ear, neither hath the eye seen, O God, beside thee, what he hath prepared for him that waiteth for him."* I want you to notice something that is very important to Paul's argument in

1Corinthians 2. The prophet is saying that although men could observe the things that God did and gave, only God observed the meaning of them, the reality that was hidden, and the substance that we now possess in Christ. According to the JFB commentary, *"The exceptive words, "O God, beside (i.e., except) thee," are not quoted directly, but virtually expressed in the exposition (1 Corinthians 2:10). "None but thou, O God, sees these mysteries: God hath revealed them to us by His Spirit. God's seeing the mysteries ensures His revealing them to His people."*[128] This verse in Isaiah 64 beautifully declares that this reality of which Paul is speaking in 1Corinthians 2, is the exclusive understanding of God, which no man can approach. Do you understand the extent of man's helplessness in context of what God has prepared and given freely to us in His Son? No wonder man would prefer to hold on to his attempts to define God's knowledge with the things that eye can see and ear can hear. What or who do you think the closest and most accessible object of that seeing and hearing would be? Bingo, it is you and me. What a deception! That is so dangerous, because unless God's exclusive sight and understanding, from which man's mind is irrevocably shut out, is revealed in us, we will convince ourselves that reality will be defined in those outwardly observable ways. Paul proposes a very dreadful situation for man. He shows his mind to be shut out and insufficient with regard to knowing what God has provided in the Son. However, thank God, He does not leave us in that state. *"But God hath revealed them unto us by His Spirit."* This is the grace and power of God on display; the revealing in our souls of the eternal substance and hidden

---

[128] Jamieson, Fausset, and Brown Commentary, Electronic Database. Copyright © 1997, 2003, 2005, 2006 by Biblesoft, Inc. All rights reserved.

wisdom of God, so that *"we might know the things that are freely given to us."*

Concerning this prepared reality and the inner work of the Spirit, Paul now expertly demonstrates the impotence of the natural man and the power of the Spirit of God. 1 Corinthians 2:10-12, *"But God hath revealed them unto us by his Spirit: for the Spirit searcheth all things, yea, the deep things of God. For what man knoweth the things of a man, save the Spirit of man which is in him? even so the things of God knoweth no man, but the Spirit of God. Now we have received, not the Spirit of the world, but the Spirit which is of God; that we might know the things that are freely given to us of God."* I do not care how many concordances deep your desk may be, how many commentaries deep your desk may be, how much you study, and how highlighted those books may be, the only one who truly searches the depths of Christ is the Spirit of Christ Himself. We search concerning His depths; the Spirit searches and thoroughly explores His depths and He alone makes those depths known by revealing Christ in us. We can and should search concerning the fullness of Christ, but the Spirit searches His fullness in reality and makes it known in us, superseding whatever study we may have done. I remember throwing away books, notebooks, and papers when I saw the Lord. I remember doing that. I disposed of them all because the revealing of Christ had already disposed of them in my heart. I was not loosing anything; I counted it all as dung because it was already seen to be dung in my heart, in the Light of the contrasting excellence of Christ.

That same thing happened in the heart of Paul. The object of reality and eternal evidence had not changed; the testimony had not changed; the object in his view had changed. He goes to those same words he read before, but now he sees Jesus, and he preached Christ from that same testimony. He did not preach Him as a coming Messiah, but as the Messiah that lives within. Christ (Messiah) in you the glory expected. He preached from the same book in which he had at one time seen himself as if it were a mirror for his natural face,[129] but now from those pages he declares the Beloved Son in whose face God's eternal satisfaction is realized. How does such a thing take place? It is due to the work of the Spirit unveiling his soul to the mystery that only God observes in the face of His Son. It is due to the work of the Spirit in his soul by which the meaning and Truth, that he sought in things which had spiritual intention, was made known in the presence of their Essential Being and source. This inward work of God is clearly set forth in these words, *"That we might know the things that are freely given to us of God. Which things also we speak, not in the words which man's wisdom teacheth, but which the Holy Ghost teacheth; comparing spiritual things with Spiritual."* As stated before, I want to focus on a portion of this verse that is seldom pointed out. It is in this portion, that I believe we see the judgment that is wrought in our hearts by the Spirit and the means by which we know the things freely given unto us.

Paul says that he and his fellow laborers declare to the Church the things that are freely given to us, but not in the wisdom of man's words. They do it as those having been taught by the Spirit of God. Paul says the same thing in

---

[129] James 1:22
Moreover, keep on becoming doers of the Word and stop being hearers only, reasoning yourselves into a false premise and thus deceiving yourselves, because if, as is the case, anyone is a hearer of the Word and not a doer, this one is like a man attentively considering in a mirror the face with which he was born. For he took one look at himself and was off, and he immediately forgot what sort of a person he was. *(from The New Testament: An Expanded Translation by Kenneth S. Wuest Copyright © 1961 by Wm. B. Eerdmans Publishing Co. All rights reserved.)*

another way in Galatians 1:11-12, *"But I certify you, brethren, that the gospel which was preached of me is not after man. For I neither received it of man, neither was I taught it, but by the revelation of Jesus Christ."* You cannot divorce the statement concerning the purpose for the Spirit being given from this next statement, which describes the means of the Spirit carrying out that purpose.

Therefore, we must examine this phrase, *"comparing spiritual things with Spiritual."* What does that mean? First, we must define the word "comparing." It is a tremendous word. It is the Greek word συγκρίνω sugkrino.[130] This word means to judge something by joining it with another thing. It also has the meaning, "to explain, primarily by means of comparison - to explain, to make clear."[131] Are you beginning to see the significance presented in these words? Let me site another source. The Jaimeson, Fausset, and Brown Commentary explains this phrase by saying that it speaks to *"expounding the Spirit-inspired Old Testament, by comparison with the gospel revealed by the same Spirit; conversely illustrating the gospel mysteries by comparing them with the Old Testament types."* Although this is a good statement, it attempts to make this merely an intellectual exercise when it is far from that. This phrase is specifically speaking of a judgment wrought in the soul by the Spirit. The Spirit of

---

[130] NT:4793 συγκρίνω sugkrino (soong-kree'-no); from NT:4862 and NT:2919; to judge of one thing in connection with another, i.e. combine (Spiritual ideas with appropriate expressions) or collate (one person with another by way of contrast or resemblance): KJV - compare among (with).
(Biblesoft's New Exhaustive Strong's Numbers and Concordance with Expanded Greek-Hebrew Dictionary. Copyright © 1994, 2003, 2006 Biblesoft, Inc. and International Bible Translators, Inc.)

[131] Greek-English Lexicon Based on Semantic Domain. Copyright © 1988 United Bible Societies, New York. Used by permission.

God thoroughly explains and perfectly discerns the eternal meaning and intention of the things of the scripture which necessitate spiritual fulfillment and brings our souls face to face with their spiritual perfection; their I AM if you will. This is far from intellect; this is a soul transforming and transitioning work of God, which we experience. We must be brought face to face with the spiritual meaning of all spiritual things.

The Law was a spiritual thing. Paul will say that. Is the Law carnal? No, it is Spiritual; I am carnal.[132] The Law is spiritual, means that it had spiritual intention and demanded a spiritual fulfillment. This means that the Law and all of this testimony had spiritual intent. There was a spiritual source, substance, and fulfillment in its view. Therefore, the Law is a spiritual thing. So what does the Spirit of God do in our hearts? The Spirit of God takes those spiritual things and compares them to what is Spiritual. He takes the things that spoke of spiritual reality and perfectly defines them by revealing their Eternal meaning and intention in our souls. The word "compare" also means to interpret. Friend, we do not need the interpretation of men when we have the perfect interpretation of the Spirit revealed in us. Such an inner interpretation wrought by the Spirit leaves no room for private interpretation. Unfortunately, most of us read concerning these spiritual things, such as righteousness, and we attempt to compare that spiritual thing or term with natural men. That is such a deceptive concept, and it will leave us blind and ignorant with regard to what God has freely given in Christ. The need is for the spiritual to be revealed, causing the evidence of that spiritual thing to be discovered in the face of the Beloved of the Father. We are

---

[132] Romans 7:14
For we know that the Law is Spiritual: but I am carnal, sold under sin.

not, nor shall we ever become, the measure or evidence of any spiritual thing. We are the habitation of the spiritual substance of all things and He must be revealed. That is the only means by which we are made to know the things that are freely given.

Interestingly, the phrase "we might know" is the same Greek word as previously used with the negative sense in the phrase, "hath not seen." The Spirit of God makes the knowledge that is impossible with man, the effectual realization of the soul. That is why 1 John 2:27 declares, *"you need not that any man teach you...for the anointing within you shall teach you all things."* This does not denigrate the need for teaching and biblical instruction. John is speaking with regard to the knowing of the full reality of salvation, it is impossible for any man to teach you. That spiritual comprehension is the work of the Spirit of Truth that abides within. May we never substitute man's instructions for the discernment of the Spirit of God being revealed within us.

Remember our consideration of these two verses. Philippians 3:6, *"Touching the righteousness which is in the Law, blameless."* Romans 7:19-21, *"For the good that I would I do not: but the evil which I would not, that I do. Now if I do that I would not, it is no more I that do it, but sin that dwelleth in me. I find then a Law, that, when I would do good, evil is present with me."* When considering daily and zealous adherence to the outward observations, he was without any blame, but when he considers the eternal meaning and intention of the Law, he realizes that his nature is entirely contrary to what the Law was after. You had a Law demanding something of your members, of you, but there was a Law in you that is contrary to the Life of which it spoke. I will not continue because we have covered this, but it spoke of a nature, a character, a spiritual and

Essential Being. It had a single intention whose coming would perfectly satisfy the Heart of the Father and we are not it. What is the answer to this dilemma? The answer is the soul being unveiled to the Very Image of the things, the spiritual certainty concerning whom the multitude of spiritual things testified.

To conclude, I want you to understand that this book came from my deep desire to see the Lord's Body come to know as we are known of God; to live in the realization of a salvation, which is far removed from our own faces and defined in the face of Christ. The unfortunate situation is that our concept of salvation is living for God by attempting to self evidence the spiritual aspects and attributes of which we read in the scriptures. However, salvation is the Life, source, and meaning of which all those things testify, living in us. It is this realization in which the Spirit of God desires we live.

He desires for us to live a life beholding the spiritual and never again attempting to define spiritual things as if they are divorced from Him and retain any aspect of Truth at all. Our journey of apprehending Christ is exclusively a work of the Spirit of God. Just as the journey depicted in Joshua, God brings before the eyes of the heart that will look, the single object of His eternal viewpoint, in order that we may pursue that view and walk in the good of our Great Salvation He has provided for us in His Son. The Father will always make known the Truth and the Truth never has the face of man as its measure or proof. The Father's view revealed in our hearts leaves no room or ground for our own familiarities. When the revealed Son is our soul's sole perspective, we can with confidence walk in pursuit of a perfection that is not outwardly observed without feeling that something is deficient. Deficiency in Christ is not a real condition, but the resulting supposition of a soul that still attempts to observe sufficiency in view of the veil of flesh. This lack of spiritual sight will thwart our pursuit for it will keep us from beholding the ark two thousand cubits before us and cause us to cast away our confidence in what God alone can reveal. Because of the deficiency of spiritual understanding, most are foolishly seeking to find the evidence of what God has given by looking at what is close to us. Most have never seen the spiritual things (love, life, righteousness, glory, power, etc.) according to God's view, so they are still expecting to discover something real in the realm of natural sight and sound. They are leaning upon their own (self-defined) understanding and thereby seeking to prove the validity of their false understanding by pointing out earthly things and defining them as heavenly. God's definition of all things prevails, but it does not prevail in our hearts, until His definition is made known. I trust it is evident that the clear division (which has been objectively wrought in the Cross) between earth and heaven, shadows and substance, illusion and reality must take place within the soul. That division is only inwardly effectual when the One who is the dividing line appears. Knowing what has been freely given includes an inward judgment that defines the perimeters in which the fullness of salvation has been given of God and must be experienced by the soul.

CHAPTER SEVEN

CAST NOT AWAY YOUR CONFIDENCE

The judgment that the Spirit of Truth works within the soul of the Christian is not what many have believed. It is not a judgment of what falls short, but it is the revealing of the Truth, which brings a clear division between the substance of Christ and the insufficiency of what falls short, which is everything else. This judgment is indeed the judgment of The Truth. It is the judgment that is brought to darkness when Light appears. It is also called the circumcision of the heart. That circumcision is, as implied, an inward severing of the soul from all that falls short of the glory of God, due to the beholding of the exceeding glory of the person of Christ, for the knowledge of that glory is only seen and found in His face. When the face of Christ comes into view, it brings a most definite division. So definite is that cutting away, that Paul said that the fullness He was beholding in Christ was the only thing that remained at all.

We have examined the crossing of Israel in Joshua 3, where they go over in view of the Ark of the Covenant of God. However, when you closely examine that story, you will notice that this pursuit of the ark will bring you to a circumcision. Joshua 5:2-3, 8-12, *"At that time the Lord said unto Joshua, Make thee sharp knives, and circumcise again the children of Israel the second time. And Joshua made him sharp knives, and circumcised the children of Israel at the hill of the foreskins... And it came to pass, when they had done circumcising all the people, that they abode in their places in the camp, till they were whole. And the Lord said unto Joshua, This day have I rolled away the reproach of Egypt from off you. Wherefore the name of the place is called Gilgal unto this day. And the children of Israel encamped in Gilgal, and kept the passover on the fourteenth day of the month at even in the plains of Jericho. And they did eat of the old corn of the land on the morrow after the passover, unleavened cakes, and parched corn in the selfsame day. And the manna ceased on the morrow after they had eaten of the old corn of the land; neither had the children of Israel manna any more; but they did eat of the fruit of the land of Canaan that year."*

What is the immediate result of this circumcision? The result is the removal of the reproach of the land and condition out from which the blood of the lamb had delivered them. I must stress that this circumcision is within the land. It was the result of beholding and following after the ark (God's Perspective: Christ). We have covered the thought of familiarity and the danger of carrying over into Christ our own familiarities. That is why this circumcision is necessary. This is what Paul calls the "circumcision of the heart."[133] The fact is this circumcision, in the Land, did not remove them from Egypt; they were already delivered from that bondage. This circumcision was to remove the remnants of Egypt from them, so that they would begin to walk in the liberty of Newness of Life that has no reference point in what has been put away or that out from which they have been delivered by God. This circumcision is the

---

[133] Romans 2:29, But he is a Jew, which is one inwardly; and circumcision is that of the heart, in the Spirit, and not in the letter; whose praise is not of men, but of God.

inward effect of the appearing of the Lord in the soul. It does not merely correct concepts that you brought with you, it removes the "I", the veil of flesh (self), in view of which you have attempted to know and define what is in the land given of God.

This circumcision removes the reproach of Egypt, the reproach of the old humanity. What can this rolling away of the reproach mean? Throughout Israel's journey, there was a constant inner relatedness to the land of bondage; the land from which they had been delivered. They seemed at times to fondly consider it as a much more pleasant situation than their current one of liberty. That is not a mystery to us. Stephen clearly defines it in Acts 7:37-39, *"This is that Moses, which said unto the children of Israel, A prophet shall the Lord your God raise up unto you of your brethren, like unto me; him shall ye hear. This is he, that was in the church in the wilderness with the angel which spake to him in the mount Sina, and with our fathers: who received the lively oracles to give unto us: To whom our fathers would not obey, but thrust him from them,* **and in their hearts turned back again into Egypt,***"* This circumcision is the answer to that. Paul defines it in a sense in Colossians 2:11, *"In whom also ye are circumcised with the circumcision made without hands, in putting off the body of the sins of the flesh by the circumcision of Christ."* It is the putting off the body of the sins of the flesh. It is putting off the entirety of one man, system, and creation, and putting on the New Man who is Christ all in all. We must face this circumcision in Christ. It is the heart forever and continually being separated in understanding and experience from the bondage of flesh and sin, self and Law. How many of us in Christ, still turn our hearts back and attempt to find something of validity in the familiarity of self and religious duty. We carry over the residual memory and relics of that which is past, attempting to make them applicable in Christ;

we must face this circumcision in the face of Christ. I do not believe that the reproach removed by this circumcision is simply the shame of having been slaves in Egypt. To me it was cutting off Egypt as a whole. In other words, this circumcision was to be an experiential forgetting of all that was behind. It was Israel partaking of the cutting off that had actually taken place in Goshen forty years previous. Do not be fooled into believing that "forgetting what is behind" is an exercise of will power. It is only the result of an effectual working of the power of God in the soul, by which you face the excellency of Christ. Then, the automatic result is the old things are passed away and removed from your soul's line of sight in the Light of the most excellent glory of the New Man. This circumcision is the remedy for the double minded, for this circumcision leaves One remaining.

We cannot know and experience what is altogether new in Christ while holding to the residue of what God has put away and out from which He has delivered us by union with the Son. It is this inward, God wrought circumcision that liberates the conscience from what is dead and cast away, unto the experiencing of a living union with the Son of God's Love. The confidence we have in Christ is directly related to the state of our conscience. We will cover the conscience in our next chapter in detail. The view of salvation that most people have is based upon what is familiar, which is due to their never having faced this clean cut.

When there has not been a clean cut in the heart, we will still believe there to be validity in past things. We will attempt to define what is of God with our natural faculties. The reality to which we have come in Christ, and are called to apprehend is not familiar. Salvation is not familiar at all. We have come, by grace, to the same situation in reality that Abraham came to in type. We have come to the land God must show unto us, for it is foreign to us.[134] We cannot know spiritual reality in the way we have known the old. We cannot know the New the way we have known the old. We cannot know the Second the way we have known the first.

Brother Sparks, in many of his books speaks of the necessity of a new set of faculties when we are concerned with the New Creation embodied in Christ. This new set of faculties is actually the inward operation of the faith of the Son of God. Faith is the faculty of a judged heart. It is the operative function of the Spirit, causing us to discover what is undiscoverable to the natural mind. Faith is the inward operation of the Spirit, by which we observe in Christ's face what we have attempted to define in our own. Therefore, it could be said that faith is truly the sign of a circumcised heart. 2 Corinthians 5:7, *"For we walk by faith, not by sight."* A heart that is not facing the judgment of which I am speaking, will always attempt to observe by sight what is only observed by faith, meaning only seen in the revealed presence of the indwelling Son. By Faith, Christ is seen and known to be the evidence and substance for which we have vainly looked in natural and external things. Here is why I say that faith is the sign of a circumcised heart. 2 Corinthians 4:18, *"While we look not at the things which are seen, but at the things which are not seen: for the things which are seen are temporal; but the things which are not seen are eternal."* This beautifully describes the activities of a heart in which faith has come and is operative. This soul, by faith, is not looking at seen, familiar, or common things and attempting to observe spiritual substance within them, but is perpetually

---

[134] Genesis 12:1

observing and laying hold of the eternal that can only be revealed of God within.

Unless we go after the ark and submit to the circumcision to which He brings us, we are going to attempt to see reality with the faculties that are only meant to see a natural creation. Therefore, because we can see it and touch it, we will immediately define that as what is real. As I presented before, this is what I believe to be the meaning of Hebrews 11:3. By faith, we understand that the things that are seen were not made by other things that are seen or are apparent, but they had eternal origin.[135] Why does he preface that by saying it is by faith we understand this? First, we must see that the writer defines faith as a means of understanding and not just a wishful thought. He says that it is by faith because if it is not the inward working of faith by which we are walking and in which we are living, we will definitely look at the seen things and think that those tangible things must be real. That false assumption keeps us ignorant and inwardly at a distance from what is real, which is the unseen fullness out from whom those seen things proceeded. Then the affection of our heart would be deviated from what is Truth, causing us to seek and look for more seen things to give us the proof and evidence of reality when the proof and the evidence is found solely in the unseen that must be revealed of God.

This brings me to what I want to cover in this chapter. As I wrote above, the confidence of the believer is directly related to his or her view of salvation. What is your view? Is it according to familiarity or is it the operation of faith

---

[135] Hebrews 11:3
Through faith we understand that the worlds came into being, and still exist, at the command of God, so that what is seen does not owe its existence to that which is visible. – Weymouth

through the revealing of God's eternal view? This verse should define for us something of the reality of our salvation. Romans 8:32, *"Indeed, He who His own Son did not spare, but on behalf of us all delivered Him up, how is it possible that He shall not with Him in grace give us all things?"*[136] I love that. How is it possible that He shall not **with Him, in grace** give us the all things? In the Greek, there is a definite article, so it is literally translated <u>the all things</u>. The small phrase "with Him" means in a living union with His Person. This is a question that needs to be posed to all believers. How is it possible that the God who showed such kindness through the death of His Son, would fail to demonstrate the same kindness to us in giving us all fullness and all spiritual blessings through our union with His Risen Son, as partakers of His Life? We read in the scripture that God will withhold no good thing from us,[137] but that is not the viewpoint in which most believers exist. Is it possible that the same God, who offered the Son up in death, would not make that same Son all things of spiritual reality unto us? How is it possible? It is not possible. God has not withheld the good thing from us. God will not withhold and has not withheld the ALL THINGS from us who seek to know Him and truly seek to pursue Him.

That is the necessary posture of your heart, if you are going to apprehend and experience the good that God has provided in His Son. You must turn to see Him. You must look unto Him. You must set the affection of your soul to

---

[136] The New Testament: An Expanded Translation by Kenneth S. Wuest Copyright © 1961 by Wm. B. Eerdmans Publishing Co. All rights reserved.

[137] Psalms 84:11-12
For the Lord God is a sun and shield: the Lord will give grace and glory: no good thing will he withhold from them that walk uprightly. O Lord of hosts, blessed is the man that trusteth in thee.

know the all things that God has freely given unto us by union with His son. How can we conceive that He has not freely given us all things in union with His Son? The JFB Commentary states this concerning Romans 8:32, *"All other gifts (all other things of salvation) being not only immeasurably less than the Gift of gifts but virtually included in it."*[138] In other words, everything else we try to get or believe God will give us (power, glory, heaven, perfection, etc) is already fully supplied and included in the presence of the gift of Christ in the soul. God has given us, in union with Himself, all things. We are not sure, it seems, of the meaning of all, so we conceive that their must at least be something of salvation that is divorced from WHO HE IS WITHIN. If our souls are set to know Him, He will be made known by the Spirit of truth, He will be made known if we pursue on to know. In other words, you will see all of these things as having already been furnished in His Life and presence. In Him, (that is Him as to His Being) the all things of your salvation have been gathered, realized, and made evident.[139]

That is something of what we are going to consider. We read in 1 Corinthians 2, that we have been given the Spirit of God so that we may know the things that have been freely given unto us. In other words, there is no way we can know it by natural means. Paul then continues to build the case concerning the impotence of the natural man with regard to spiritual reality. What are the *"all thing that have been freely given"* if not what he defines in the first chapter, Christ in us made unto us all things of Life and

---

[138] Jamieson, Fausset, and Brown Commentary, Electronic Database. Copyright © 1997, 2003, 2005, 2006 by Biblesoft, Inc. All rights reserved.

[139] Reference the etymology of the word satisfied as described in the Preface of this book.

Godliness; the all that we, in our religious ignorance, attempt to acquire by whatever means we deem necessary. In reality, God has given us all things in the Son. The Spirit of God now works upon that premise in order to make His fullness the experience of our hearts and not merely the theological conviction of our brains.

That work requires a heart that is in a posture set to know Him. God desires for the soul that He created to know the One whose inheritance it is. He will not share His perspective to those who are not solely looking for Him, who are deviated in any way. So many Christians, due to a supposition of lack, are seeking additions to Him, and supplements for what we deem to be a lack in our salvation. I promise you, if we see Him, we will understand that everything God has given is embodied in His already present Life. That is why it is essential for the Spirit of God to take spiritual things and compare them with their spiritual substance who inhabits our souls. The Spirit of God unveils our souls to the spiritual intention of all things and declares Him to be the exegesis of the Father's heart and will within.[140] The Spirit expounds inwardly the eternal meaning of **the all things** of the testimony. Here is when the soul is made to see what is incapable of being seen, to observe the hidden wisdom of God. The Spirit of Truth makes known that the elements of the testimony do not

---

[140] John 1:18
No one has seen God at any time; the only begotten God who is in the bosom of the Father, He **has explained** Him. – NASU

NT:1834 ἐξηγέομαι exegeomai (ex-ayg-eh'-om-ahee); *(Biblesoft's New Exhaustive Strong's Numbers and Concordance with Expanded Greek-Hebrew Dictionary. Copyright © 1994, 2003, 2006 Biblesoft, Inc. and International Bible Translators, Inc.)*

Author's Note: This is the word from which our English word exegesis is derived. Christ is the exegesis or full exposition of the Father.

have a separate measurement or identity apart from Christ. This is when we behold the "all things" that God has not withheld from us. This work of the Spirit of God truly severs our souls from all of the foolishness we have attempted to identify as spiritual knowledge.

Most of us look at things and we evaluate those things and then we make a judgment based on the things we see, but the fact is, if we are truly judged inwardly, we do not go to those things and make judgments based on what we see naturally. We go in the midst of those seen things having already been judged in the Light of the Spiritual. We are already severed from those things. So those things are already judged in our heart as having no benefit or validity at all and in that state, we are incapable of becoming victim to or the spoil of the vain philosophies of man. Galatians 6:14, *"But God forbid that I should glory, save in the Cross of our Lord Jesus Christ, by whom the world is crucified unto me, and I unto the world."* He did not have to go to every element of the Old Covenant age and look at them in order to make assessments as to whether they were good or not. He was dead to it. He was judged. His heart was circumcised. If we ever see Christ, we will see that these things have already been judged as nothing. Paul did not give up anything of value in the seeing of Christ, he just saw it for what it was and released it. He understood that, just as the camp of Israel, to keep the dung within the camp would have corrupted and contaminated it. It had to be taken out of the city or out of the camp, out of the encampment, burned and buried. Most of us are holding onto dung. This is due to an absence of the seeing of Christ. The Spirit of God is constantly calling our hearts unto a heavenly view. Come up hither – come and see the reality I have already given you. Come, see my satisfaction, and cease looking for it in yourself or anywhere else.

Hebrews 13:9, *"Be not carried about with divers and strange doctrines. For it is a good thing that the heart be established with grace; not with meats, which have not profited them that have been occupied therein."* Outward observances and religious activities have never profited a soul that has been occupied in them. Has any religious observance, by which you have attempted to please God, transformed your soul? The answer is no of course. But so many of us still look back toward those things as if they did profit us in some way. Paul will tell us that he was wholeheartedly convinced that He was serving God by doing things contrary to the name of Jesus; that is until Jesus appeared. The fact is, we may not be hunting down Christians and putting them in prison, but we are still occupying our time in that which is contrary to the reality we have in Christ. Just as with Paul, the remedy for that deception is SEEING JESUS. So many of us still look in the earth for something that will not profit the soul. What is lacking? What causes us to seek in vain? There is the absence of an inner solidity. That is another phrase for the word "established." This inner solidity only comes when the soul is unveiled to the Truth. It is the solidity of faith, whereby your soul is secured in the reality of what is revealed of the Father in the face of His Son. This is what Hebrews calls *"an anchor of the soul, both sure and stedfast, and which entereth into that within the veil."*[141]

Faith is the anchor that keeps us securely fixed in the "all things" we have been given IN HIM IN GRACE. That steadfastness of heart keeps us from diverting our gaze toward something familiar; what is perceivable by the faculties of the natural man. There must be this inward establishing. Where the knowing of the Truth or the seeing of Christ is not present, we immediately assume something

---

[141] Hebrews 6:19

of fullness to be absent. However, the fact is that we are purely ignorant of its reality, for we are ignorant of the presence of Christ. We devise means or methods by which to acquire or to exhibit those spiritual things that we deem to be lacking. The only reason they seem to be lacking is that we are attempting to see the evidence and the proof of them with the faculties that were never meant to see the evidence and proof.

We feel the need to add. We think there is insufficient proof or we think there is a need to attach externalities, works, or efforts because the evidence for which we long appears to be absent. However, the evidence of spiritual reality is not seen or known in the same way it was in an Old Covenant or Creation. It is not the proof or the evidence that is insufficient; it is the faculties with which we are attempting to observe that evidence. They are insufficient. They cannot know the proof that is already present in us. Since seeing Christ, my prayer has not been that the Lord would bring His fullness into the earth, so I can grasp it intellectually. My prayer is let faith appear. Let my soul, by faith, be continually experiencing the eternal evidence and living proof of salvation who lives within, the evidence that will never be exhibited in any earthly way.

It seems that most of us are seeking for God to bring reality into the earth. Romans 10:6-8, *"But the righteousness which is of faith speaketh on this wise, Say not in thine heart, Who shall ascend into heaven? (that is, to bring Christ down from above:) Or, Who shall descend into the deep? (that is, to bring up Christ again from the dead.) But what saith it? The word is nigh thee, even in thy mouth, and in thy heart: that is, the word of faith, which we preach."* Nothing of reality is afar off from us. Christ, who is the righteousness of faith, is in us. You do not have to bring Him down, or bring Him up as if He is in another place. He is in you. The Word of Faith is in you. We are ignorant of the righteousness of God, therefore we insist on going about to establish our own righteousness. I guarantee you, just as with the Galatians, it will be an external righteousness, an externally evidenced righteousness because we want it to be something we can see, something we can understand.

However, I must repeat, salvation is not familiar territory. It must be seen in the light of the ark. Reality must be revealed of God in the soul. The evidence of salvation will never be given in external or outward ways. God did that under the age of the testimony because nothing of reality, at that time, could indwell the heart of man. However, there were those who, by faith, observed a reality that was greater than the seen things. They saw, afar off, spiritual evidence that would come in Christ that was not made evident by the things they were able to see. It is by Faith, in the New Covenant, that we observe inwardly the reality and evidence, which they saw afar off. They saw it as a coming promise, but we see Him in whom the promise is yes and amen.

Grace has brought us nigh to the reality they saw afar off. The need, again, is for the soul to be established with and in the grace of God that has made such union a reality. Another word study commentary says that the meaning of the word established here is *"to cause something to be known as certain - to confirm, to verify, to prove to be true and certain."*[142] The revealing of the Son brings the confirming proof of our Great Salvation into the soul. This anchor makes it possible for us to enjoy and experience our salvation so that it would in no way be dependent upon the

---

[142] Greek-English Lexicon Based on Semantic Domain. Copyright © 1988 United Bible Societies, New York. Used by permission.

variableness and ever-changing nature of people, external events, outward manifestations, or observable occurrences. That is where most seem to be looking. The Truth is never found in that which varies from day to day and from time to time.

Our souls must be as the city in Revelation; they should have no need for natural light or natural evidence. That need still exists when the soul remains ignorant of the evidence that is revealed in the face of Jesus Christ. He must be the Light of it. He must be the sight of it. He must be the perspective of our souls. When He is not the perspective of our hearts, we can actually be convinced that there is some validity in the seen things. That is a state the letter of Hebrews calls "an evil conscience."

That is the reason for a warning I want to consider in Hebrews chapter 10. We all know what is written in the first part of that chapter. The writer is establishing the reality that Christ came as the end of the first, in which God had no pleasure, and was brought forth by God as the Life and fullness of the Second. The Second is the Son raised and living as the pleasure and satisfaction of God in our hearts. Everything in this chapter is according to that beautiful narrative. However, I want to focus on the following portion of this chapter. Hebrews 10:32-35, *"But call to remembrance the former days, in which, after ye were illuminated, ye endured a great fight of afflictions; Partly, whilst ye were made a gazingstock both by reproaches and afflictions; and partly, whilst ye became companions of them that were so used. For ye had compassion of me in my bonds, and took joyfully the spoiling of your goods, knowing in yourselves that ye have in heaven a better and an enduring substance. Cast not away therefore your confidence, which hath great recompence of reward."* Notice this. For ye had compassion on me in my bonds and took joyfully the spoiling of your goods knowing in yourselves that ye have in heaven a better and an enduring substance. First, it must be pointed out that the phrase "in heaven" is not found in the original text. It does not change the meaning of the verse if it were there, assuming we have a grasp of what it means to be in heaven, but I did at least feel the need to point that out. The actual reading should be "you took joyfully the spoiling of your goods for you know in yourselves that you have a better and an enduring substance." You know inwardly that you possess, in Christ, something greater, something better, something more eternally significant than even the natural things that have been taken from you or destroyed. You realize that you have something greater, you have a better and a more enduring substance. We know that substance is Christ in you. He will progress in the next chapter and make it clear that such substance is only seen and apprehended by faith.[143]

The writer of the letter is reminding them of the assurance in which they walked after they came to comprehend the New Covenant that had come in Christ. So he writes, *"Cast not away therefore your confidence, which hath great recompence of reward. For ye have need of patience, that, after ye have done the will of God, ye might receive the promise."* We must consider this within the context of this letter. These people are living under threat and persecution to return to an outward obedience to the Mosaic Law. The writer is saying to them, at one point in time you understood and you comprehended that the better substance, the enduring substance you possess is a heavenly

---

[143] Hebrews 11:1
Now faith is the substance of things hoped for, the evidence of things not seen.

and spiritual substance. You had something better and you knew it. Therefore, do not cast away your confidence that is according to that substance. It occurs to me that this is a much more serious problem than we may think. It has to do with casting aside your inward assurance with regard to an unseen substance, which is only observed by faith.

Do not cast that confidence away for it brings and has great recompense of reward. In other words, do not be deceived to look in the externals for eternal substance. Stop allowing people to cause your heart to look outside of Christ for anything. Stop allowing them to divert your heart's attention from that unseen God-revealed reality to something that the eye can see, the ear can hear, and the mind can understand. Do not allow this, for your continuation in this confidence has great reward. It truly has riches and wealth. It will cause your soul to partake of the unsearchable riches of Christ.

As it reads in Proverbs 8:21, *"To cause my lovers to inherit substance, Yea, their treasures I fill."*[144] That is the substance of which the writer is speaking. The greater substance they already have. He is saying to them, "In view of that greater substance, in view of the fact that you have been brought into this reality of the Second and are in union with the Risen Son, why would you cast away your confidence in that and again look to these external things?" It is as if Paul is saying, "Why would you seek to be bound by the rudiments and elements of this Mosaic age, when you have been given the liberty of the Law of the Life and presence of the Spirit of the Son."[145] The writer is saying

---

[144] Young's Literal Translation

[145] Galatians 5:1
Stand fast therefore in the liberty wherewith Christ hath made us free, and be not entangled again with the yoke of bondage.

very much the same thing as Paul in Colossians 2:18 *"Let no man beguile you of your reward."* Cast not away your confidence for it has great recompense of reward. In other words, let no man beguile you of your reward or deceive or attempt to disqualify you from your present reward (the riches of Christ's presence) who says that you do not get the reward because you are no longer occupying yourselves in these external things or the seen things. Does this make sense? Let no man deviate your heart from the body, the substance that Christ is. All they will do is rob you of a present prize. This is so much more serious than having your natural possessions plundered. This has to do with the soul missing an experiential participation with the Second, the eternal substance due to being deceived to look back at what is familiar, what is behind. I have seen this type of regression many times.

So what is the answer or the necessity that is presented? It is presented in both Colossians 3 and Hebrews 10. Hebrews 10:36, *"For ye have need of patience, that, after ye have done the will of God, ye might receive the promise."* What is the answer to the seeming lack of reality, the answer to the false suppositions of the natural mind, which cause us to turn back to familiar ground? The answer is not to cast away your confidence. The answer is to assume a posture of absolute dependence upon the Spirit of Truth. The answer is PATIENCE! When something of salvation seems to be

---

Colossians 2:8-10
Beware lest any man spoil you through philosophy and vain deceit, after the tradition of men, after the rudiments of the world, and not after Christ. For in him dwelleth all the fulness of the Godhead bodily. And ye are complete in him, which is the head of all principality and power.

Colossians 2:20
Wherefore if ye be dead with Christ from the rudiments of the world, why, as though living in the world, are ye subject to ordinances.

missing, the answer is not to turn your view back into the earth and back into the external things in order to find it there. Colossians 3:1-2, *"If ye then be risen with Christ, seek those things which are above, where Christ sitteth on the right hand of God. Set your affection on things above, not on things on the earth."* Looking back into the earth, back into the shadows in order to observe and discover spiritual substance is not the answer. The answer is patience with a heart set on that which is above. The need is patience. It is a continual inward looking and waiting for the appearing of the substance of the Second. Patience is not waiting on a substance that is not present. This patience is waiting unto the inward appearing of the One who is the embodiment of that better and enduring substance. That is the need for the believer. Patience! The writer of Hebrews presents this journey of faith, this pursuit of Christ, as a race. How are we, who have come to the "BETTER THINGS" for which these in Hebrews 11 looked, to pursue? Hebrews 12:1, *"And let us run with patience the race that is set before us."* This journey demands patience. We have come to the better things provided of God. We have come to the spiritual fullness for which an entire age waited. It is altogether New, for it is of God and not of us. The salvation given of God is spiritual. We have come to the spiritual confirmation of the faith of those numbered in Hebrews 11. Not one thing they saw afar off, by faith, was fulfilled by external or natural things. That means the salvation we have is entirely spiritual, meaning that it is given and worked within us by the Spirit of God.[146] We cannot have it or grow in the knowledge of it, except by the inward operation of the Spirit taking of Christ and openly showing it to the soul.

---

[146] John 16:15
All things that the Father hath are mine: therefore said I, that he shall take of mine, and shall shew it unto you.

The need for us who are come to Zion, the mountain that cannot be touched (not physical or material), is patience. We must patiently wait for the appearing, in our souls, of the Author and the Finisher of Faith, so that we may know the glorious fullness that is entirely embodied in His presence. It is patience unto the coming of the Lord, but in an inward soul-transforming manner. This is the patience which carries with it the benefit of profound riches. That reward is the experiencing of the appearing and abiding presence of Christ and apprehending Him as the personification of all spiritual blessing. The lack of patience ensures our returning to and our continued occupation with the idols of our own familiarity.

Paul addresses this need in Galatians 5:5, *"For we through the Spirit wait for the hope of righteousness by faith."* He prefaces this with *"Christ is become of no effect unto you, whosoever of you are justified by the Law; ye are fallen from grace."* If we seek righteousness outside of the union wherein Christ is made unto us all things, we have severed ourselves from Christ. We are attempting to relate to God in a manner in which He does not relate. We are seeking, out of our ignorance, to establish our own standing with God, which will bear our own image. This is the terrible result of impatience: ISHMAEL! Abraham had no animus toward God's promise, he believed God, but he would not wait on the TIME OF LIFE. He took it into His own hands to produce what could only be done and provided of God in His Seed. Lack of patience will produce Ishmael. We will attempt to go back to familiar ground in order to help God produce something that He has already provided and fully supplied in union with His Son. Paul says, we through the Spirit, we by the power of the Spirit working within, do wait with unshakable expectation upon the inner appearing of the righteousness of God Himself. In His appearing, we are no longer permitted to seek a righteousness that falls short. This patience is unto the appearing of Christ in the soul, as the spiritual perfection of the spiritual things of the testimony. If we are not patient unto that end, we will continue to take those spiritual things and bring them unto ourselves in order to define or evidence them. There is no "recompense of reward" in that, only condemnation.

It is a dangerous thing and a great bondage to know true things, even spiritual things, and never see the Truth of those things. To know that righteousness is the requirement of God, but never behold inwardly the One who is the righteousness of God is bondage. If that is the state of our comprehension, we are going to attempt to produce the evidence of what we understand to be the promise. It is never going to work, it is bondage. So you have need of patience. Again, this patience is not for God to fulfill anything that is lacking with regard to completeness, but for the revealing of Christ as the completeness of all things.

James 1:4, *"But let patience have her perfect work, that ye may be perfect and entire, wanting nothing."* What is the perfect work of patience? To read this on the surface would cause you to thing that the perfect work of patience is the acquiring of what is lacking, but it is not at all. The perfect work of patience is the appearing in the soul of the Perfect Man in whom nothing is lacking at all. He appears as the reality of our present state of being. Our confidence is only shaken and cast aside when we are ignorant of our present state of fullness in Christ. However, His appearing makes known and makes manifestly clear the Truth of our salvation. Therefore, the perfect work of patience does not MAKE you perfect, entire and wanting nothing. His appearing makes that a manifest comprehension of the soul. Christ appears to the patient soul, that is unshakably set on what is above as the soul's salvation, which is perfect, entire and has nothing at all lacking within itself.

This is no better typified than on the Day of Atonement. On this day, the High Priest would enter behind the veil. He would stand before the Lord with the white linen garments and the mitre on his head that declared: Holiness unto the Lord. This demonstrated that only the Head is accepted by the Father. There is much to this, but I cannot tackle that at this time. While the High Priest stood in the presence of God and was accepted in the sight of God, the people of Israel were commanded to stand outside of the door of the tabernacle and wait upon his return from the Holiest. They were to wait on him. They could not see him and they did not know the condition of their standing with God as long as he remained hidden from their sight. Their confidence could indeed have waned as they waited expectantly for him. However, the only answer to such a condition of questions concerning the security of their relationship with God came when he appeared before them. They knew that their salvation was secured because He was living in their midst, but that knowledge came only in his appearing. Their patience had its perfect work in his appearing and they saw in him a salvation with nothing missing and nothing deficient.[147] His revealed presence brought with it the great reward of comprehending salvation as God comprehends it in the person of their High Priest.[148] The perfection,

---

[147] "While the High Priest was in the Most Holy Place in the very presence of God, the people meantime with mounting tension waited for the reappearance of the High Priest, in dreadful fear lest his prolonged absence in the Holy of Holies signify that God had not forgiven His people and had slain their unworthy High Priest. When at last the High Priest came out of the Most Holy Place, the people sighed with relief that their service was accepted, and their sins forgiven." – *excerpt from The Gospel in the Feast of Israel by Victor Buksbazen (pg. 38 publisher The Friends of Israel Gospel Ministry, Inc.)*

[148] 1 Corinthians 13:10-12
But when that which is perfect is come, then that which is in part shall be done away. When I was a child, I spake as a child, I understood as a child, I thought as a child: but when I became a man, I put away childish things.

entireness, and presence of their atonement was made known in him. What was true in the Holiest was seen to be Truth in his unveiled presence. What was unknown to be reality due to a veil, was now known in his unveiled presence.

This is the meaning of the next statement. Hebrews 10:36, *"For ye have need of patience, that, after ye have done the will of God, ye might receive the promise."* After ye have done the will of God is a very bad translation. It brings works of the flesh back into central focus. It gives us the idea that we now have to fulfill the will of God, but that is not the case. The more literal rendering of it is *"the will of God being done."* Is that not the point of the first verses of Chapter 10? *"Lo, I come to do* (fulfill completely) *thy will O God."* So the writer is saying, your need of patience is so that, the will of God being done, you might receive the promise. That is why you need patience. It is only through this patience that you truly receive the promise. Again, this does not mean that they do not already have the promise, but that by patience unto His coming, they will experience the reality that was promised and is now provided in the Son. The word receiving here means to cause someone to experience something on the basis of it having already been done, to cause them to experience something already done.[149] You need patience that the will of God being done, you might receive the promise. In His appearing, the soul is made to experience the reality that is already done and perfectly provided by union with Christ.

For now we see through a glass, darkly; but then face to face: now I know in part; but then shall I know even as also I am known.

[149] NT:2865 κομίζω to cause someone to experience something on the basis of what that person has already done. *(from Greek-English Lexicon Based on Semantic Domain. Copyright © 1988 United Bible Societies, New York. Used by permission.)*

The promise we receive is not another promise of something better to come. Remember, this entire thing is based upon the fact that they have a better and enduring substance. The patience is unto their souls being made perfectly aware of the substance that they have. The word promise here *"speaks of **the thing promised** and so signifies a gift graciously **bestowed**, not a pledge."*[150] This is important. It is acceptable to speak of the covenant as a contract. Therefore, what fulfills a contract that makes a promise? We call that a promissory note. What fulfills that contract? Is it fulfilled with another contract making more promises or is it fulfilled when what was promised is present? That is the promise we receive when He appears in our souls. We see and lay hold of the content of the promise. We apprehend, in Light, the substance and fullness that God promised to the fathers. That is the point being made here. Do not cast away your confidence, do not look in the earth for the reality of these spiritual things, and do not be deceived to look again toward these externalities. You need patience; you need to set the affection of your heart unto the appearing of Christ.

This is the same answer he gives in Colossians 3. Colossians 3:1-4, *"If ye then be risen with Christ, seek those things which are above, where Christ sitteth on the right hand of God. Set your affection on things above, not on things on the earth. For ye are dead, and your life is hid with Christ in God. When Christ, who is our life, shall appear, then shall ye also appear with him in glory."* How was the confidence of the Colossians being shaken? They were being deceived to look outside of their present union with Christ and back to the earthly elements of the Old in order to realize something of reality. Their need was not to

---

[150] Vine's Expository Dictionary of Biblical Words, Copyright © 1985, Thomas Nelson Publishers.

seek for natural evidence based upon a real ignorance with regard to spiritual Truth. Their need, as those risen with Christ, was to set the affection of their hearts, the gaze of the soul above and patiently await the appearing of Christ their Life. When Christ the Life of God, the Life we have as born again believers, appears, then what has been a reality from the beginning (new birth) is made apparent to the soul. We see in His presence what has been the actual state of our souls. The problem is not the presence of reality, but our ignorance of the reality present. The reality that has existed since the moment He came and indwelt your heart will be made apparent in His appearing. It is in this appearing we experience the inward circumcision of the heart and are in Truth severed from all external observance and earthly evidences.

So, we have the next statement, which must be understood in context. In context it cannot mean what futurists attempt to make it mean. Hebrews 10:37, *"For yet a very very little, He who is coming will come, and will not tarry."*[151] Notice the present tense of what is made to sound futuristic in the King James. *"He who is coming will come"*. This is not about dispensations. This speaks of the ever coming nature of Christ our Life unto the soul that will look for Him.[152] The writer is quoting the prophet Habakkuk, but he is not presenting this as a promise for a coming time. He is declaring unto them the fulfillment of Habakkuk's prophecy in the inward appearing of Christ unto the patient soul. *"Yet a little while and He that shall come will come."* "Shall come" is in the present tense. To the soul expectantly

---

[151] Young's Literal Translation

[152] Hebrews 9:28
So Christ also, having been offered once to bear the sins of many, will appear a second time for salvation without reference to sin, to those who eagerly await Him. – New American Standard Updated

awaiting his appearing, Christ will continue in His coming and in that coming the soul will experience the content of what has been promised. Cast not away your confidence. Set your heart patiently upon His coming.

Hebrews 4:1, *"Let us therefore fear lest, a promise at anytime being left behind and still remaining of entering His rest, anyone of you should think that he has fallen short of it or has come too late."*[153] Instead of "should think" the King James Version reads, "should seem." That is very important in the understanding of this passage as well as the New Covenant itself. The fear addressed here is not a fear of actually missing or coming short of the rest promised of God. The writer knows that to be impossible if they are already in Christ. They have come to the rest of God in Christ. The fear that is presented is the fear of a false supposition that causes them to believe that they have indeed come short of the promise of God. This false supposition is the reason for the casting away of our confidence in the spiritual reality. It is because the majority is attempting to understand the rest of God, the salvation in Christ, with the mind of flesh and not with the mind of the Spirit. When that false supposition is present, it is proof that we are attempting to know salvation in a way in which it cannot be known. That is the reason the majority of Christians hold to some future timeline theology. It is much easier to push reality off to some undetermined time in the future than it is to wait patiently on the appearing of Christ. No, if you will not cast away your confidence and you will set your heart patiently, He will appear. In His appearing, you will receive or comprehend in Light, the content of the promise of which you **seemed** at one time to come short. It seemed at one time you had come short of this promise.

---

[153] Kenneth Wuest Translation

You may presently be in that state of assumption. However, if you will patiently wait for His appearing, He will come and you will see Him to be the very content of all things promised. You will see Him to be the Yes and the Amen of all the promises of God.[154] In the Light of His countenance, we do not have to look in the earth or to ourselves for proof; we do not have to look in the earth for evidence. We do not need it. The eternal proof, eternal evidence and content of all promises has appeared. The revealing of the Son in the soul needs no further evidence. Therefore, set your affection on things above.

I end this chapter by asking a simple question. As those who are risen with Christ, as those who have been given all things in union with Christ, as those who are indwelt with the Spirit of the eternal pleasure and satisfaction of the Father; what is the state of your confidence? Is your confidence demanding patience unto His coming or do you now have confidence in the flesh to produce the result you believe to be lacking? Patience is demanded from the soul that will behold the full satisfaction and pleasure of the Father. Cast not away your confidence; set your heart patiently upon His appearing so that in His Light, in the light of faith, the promise will be known as sure to the soul.[155]

---

[154] 2 Corinthians 1:20
For all the promises of God in him are yea, and in him Amen, unto the glory of God by us.

[155] Romans 4:16
Therefore it is of faith, that it might be by grace; to the end the promise might be sure to all the seed; not to that only which is of the Law, but to that also which is of the faith of Abraham; who is the father of us all,

CHAPTER EIGHT

THE ANSWER OF A GOOD CONSCIENCE

I ended the last chapter asking about the condition of your confidence. The question could actually be asked, "In whose face are you expecting to see the evidence of spiritual fullness and perfection?" The answer you give to this question determines where your confidence lies. As stated before, the realm in which your confidence is set is directly determined by the state of your conscience. I want to deal with the conscience in this chapter.

When is reality real? When is truth true? The answers to these questions are obvious. Reality is always reality. Truth is always truth. These things are fixed and cannot change. Therefore, in the heart of most believers the problem is perspective. The problem is where we are attempting to find that fixed reality. Our problem is that most of us believe that reality lies in the realm of the external. Most believe that reality is defined by what is visible to the natural eye and seen in the realm of sight and sound. However, that is not the case at all. Reality has been eternally before the face of God and is His **exclusive** point of view. Does our ignorance make eternal reality less real? That is a ludicrous thought. In fact, it was out from that eternal reality that every person, place, and testimonial element was created and brought into being. If it was not for that eternal reality that was hidden from the sight and understanding of natural man, and that stood in the sight of God before there was a man, nothing that was made would have been made. There would not have been a type, there would not have been a figure, there would not have been one word spoken. God created all of these things to testify of One eternal reality. Christ being born of a woman into the world did not make Him anything. The invisible eternal substance taking on a visible form and relating to natural men, did not make Him more than what He had eternally been. He came AS who He had eternally been. Not one thing that He did that was visible to the natural eye displayed who He actually was. He stood as eternal reality in the midst of religious imaginations.

It can be said that the dark mind of the natural men to whom He came could not comprehend the Light of His Eternal Being.[156] This is evidently set forth in Matthew 16:13-17. *"When Jesus came into the coasts of Caesarea Philippi, he asked his disciples, saying, Whom do men say that I the Son of man am? And they said, Some say that thou art John the Baptist: some, Elias; and others, Jeremias, or one of the prophets. He saith unto them, But whom say ye that I am? And Simon Peter answered and said, Thou art the Christ, the Son of the living God. And Jesus answered and said unto him, Blessed art thou, Simon Barjona: for flesh and blood hath not revealed it unto thee, but my Father which is in heaven."* The people had seen the

---

[156] John 1:5
And the light in the darkness did shine, and the darkness did not **perceive** it. – Young's Literal Translation

NT:2638 καταλαμβάνω   (a figurative extension of meaning of καταλαμβάνω d 'to overcome,' 37.19) to come to understand something which was not understood or perceived previously - 'to understand, to realize, to grasp, to comprehend.' *(Greek-English Lexicon Based on Semantic Domain. Copyright © 1988 United Bible Societies, New York. Used by permission.)*

things Jesus did and had heard His beautiful words, however that never caused them to perceive who He was in their midst. The reality of His Eternal Person was hidden from their understanding; that was God's exclusive view and understanding. Natural men observed what He did and, based upon that, they attempted to assess who He was. They made assumptions based on their natural concepts and even their religious traditions. It may appear that their assumptions were very spiritual because they were talking about dead people coming back from the dead. It may sound deep and intense, but it was nothing more than natural minds grasping at straws in order to identify what was beyond their ability to know. The fact is, they had no idea who He was because it was still based on their outward observance of flesh and blood. The understanding of flesh and blood can only go as deep as flesh and blood. Who was it that truly comprehended the Light that stood in their midst? It was the one unto whom the Father made Him known by revelation. Do you see this? Peter's comprehension of Jesus went beyond natural perception and religious background. This was not Peter's own understanding. God made HIS OWN understanding known unto Peter. Jesus tells Peter that flesh and blood did not reveal that understanding to Him. What we must see is that even when Jesus was visible to the natural eye, WHO HE WAS could never be perceived in that way. This must also be understood in the light of our Great Salvation. As long as we are bound to our own understanding and the insufficiency of our perceptive faculties, it will be impossible to know the fixed and eternal reality that Christ is.

Therefore, reality is always reality; truth is always truth, but when does reality become the realization in us? Does it become real in us when we see it, as they say, walked out in shoe leather, or is it real in us when we see it in the face of Jesus Christ? That is why I said in the previous chapter, the revelation of Jesus Christ requires no further evidence. Reality must be made known inwardly; the soul must be established in grace by faith. The soul must be anchored in the unseen and eternal. I am not discounting our outward activities as those who are beholding reality, such as outreach and ministry. The problem is when we attempt to define the proof of spiritual reality by those outward things. Outward things must proceed from the inward beholding of reality. The proof must be found inwardly, by the revelation of Christ, for that is the only place proof and evidence can be found. That is why the coming of faith has to take place.

Romans 8:32, *"Indeed, He who His own Son did not spare, but on behalf of us all delivered Him up, how is it possible that He shall not with Him in grace give us all things?"*[157] Everything of our salvation is given by union with the Son; there is nothing given to us of God that is not found within the confines of His Son. In fact, His Son is the all things that God gives. The problem is we attempt to comprehend the all things He has given with the wrong faculties. They are never observable or perceivable in that way. That is why God must reveal His Son. If God does not reveal His Son we are shut out as far as knowing the salvation we have been given.

Unfortunately, most of us are occupied with the vanity of looking in the earth for reality, and that is why most are casting away their confidence. Many think there is a lack somewhere in Christ, so they automatically cast away their confidence in the sufficiency of Christ, and look for something true and perfect in a false realm. If our heart has not been rooted, grounded, and established in Truth by

---

[157] The New Testament: An Expanded Translation by Kenneth S. Wuest Copyright © 1961 by Wm. B. Eerdmans Publishing Co. All rights reserved.

faith, we are going to be in a constant state of searching. God is not searching for anything. As I have stated before, God's view and understanding is eternally fixed. Why is it that our hearts are searching for more, longing for something better? Very simple, God's fixed view is not being revealed in us. Our need is not to expect God to bring something more substantial into being at a future date. It is not to believe that He will cause us to be better than we are. According to the writer of the letter to the Hebrews, the greatest need for the soul of the believer is patience unto the appearing of the Lord. Why waste time attempting to peer back into unprofitable externalities in order to find benefit? The only benefit to the soul is it being unveiled to the fixed and eternal satisfaction of the Father. Our ultimate need is to see Jesus in an inward way.

When I make that statement to some people, they seem to get frustrated with me. They think I am pushing them off and attempting to avoid giving an answer to whatever question they may be asking. I do care about people understanding things and I will take time to talk to people when they have questions. However, the only answer that will satisfy the soul is not going to come from me or any other external source. The answer that will satisfy the soul is Christ revealed. He is the Truth and nothing else is. The answer is not looking in the earth for something or trying to define what God is doing by what happens in the earth, the answer is seeing the Lord.

As I have considered the things that have been presented in this book, the Lord has truly been bringing a clear distinction in my heart about what is earthly and what is heavenly, what is Spirit and what is flesh. Such a clear cut is only brought about as Christ crucified goes from an event that took place at a certain point in time, to an ever present inward work of the Spirit judging between the dead and the

Living One. How many of us are still "seeking the Living One among the death and darkness of humanity?" We carry over into Christ the remnants of a destroyed creation and a dead man. Brother Sparks calls this the danger of the carry over. Brother Sparks writes, *"The tragedy is because of a carry over of that old rejected and discredited humanity into the realm of the New. This is a terrible tragedy. It is a great tragedy when you ignore that great gap that God has placed by the Cross, between one humanity and Another (Christ), when you do not recognize how utter the cleavage which the Cross has made. In our hearts, there is a carry over of relics and remnants of an old humanity. There is something of the New, but there has been a carry over of the Old in the Christian Life; the result: confusion – confusion in judgment, confusion in behavior, confusion in relationships."*[158]

Confusion is rampant in the Church world today. Yet, we read very clearly that God is not the author of confusion. So what is the source of the confusion that is so evident? The answer can even be found in the etymology of the word confusion. The Greek word for confusion[159] means disorder and instability. That definition is further solidified when you understand that it also has its origin in the Latin word *confundere*. That word actually means a mingling together, pouring, and blending together. This sheds light on the instability of most Christians. The problem is not that we have not found the secret to making the flesh and the Spirit co-labor, in order to produce the results we think please

---

[158] Excerpts from *The Great Transition from One Humanity to Another* by T. Austin Sparks [www.austin-sparks.net]

[159] NT:181 ἀκαταστασία akatastasia (ak-at-as-tah-see'-ah); from NT:182; instability, i.e. disorder: KJV - commotion, confusion, tumult. *(Biblesoft's New Exhaustive Strong's Numbers and Concordance with Expanded Greek-Hebrew Dictionary. Copyright © 1994, 2003, 2006 Biblesoft, Inc. and International Bible Translators, Inc.)*

God. The problem is that in our hearts two things still exist to be mingled together. Do you see this? The Cross has not left two things; the Cross does not leave Jesus and a better person. The Cross leaves One living in the soul of all who will live. When we comprehend, by the revealing of Christ, that One who lives and remains, there is no more room for confusion. We cannot mingle or fuse together two things when only One remains. That is the judgment, the circumcision of the heart. It cuts away, from our soul's sight, all that we have attempted to carry over.

Those things divert the orientation of the heart and keep it bound to the earth. If your heart is bound to the earth and your comprehension of salvation is not the result of the inward transition from earth to heaven, your confidence with regard to salvation will be in view of the earth, even the earthly pursuits of religion that are performed by earthly men. Your confidence is going to be found again in that which is natural, external, and observable to the natural man. The writer of the Hebrew letter says you do not need to look at the earth again; we do not need to attempt to define something of the New within the external things. We need patience. Instead of trying to figure something out or saying here is what I believe God desires or what satisfies His heart, we need patience unto the appearing in our hearts of the substance of His delight.

The ever coming Christ will continue in His coming to the soul that is continually and patiently set unto His appearing. That is why you need patience. In that appearing, we will receive the content of the promise of the Father. In His inward appearing, the reality that Christ is already made unto us as the fulfillment of all the promises of God will be made manifestly apparent in us. This will allow us actively to apprehend what we have ignorantly believed to be lacking due to the state of blindness that would not permit our hearts to see anything of reality removed from ourselves.

Christ will appear as the Living One in whom all things are Yes and Amen and in whom the Father is glorified. The taking away of the first and the Second that is established will be an inward reality effecting a true separation. This separation, the inward effect of the Cross, will cause the soul to be joined to the reality established in Christ and severed from that, which is done away. What is truly done away by the Cross? What does the inward effect of the Cross remove from our hearts? The veil of flesh was done away by the Cross and that same veil of flesh is taken away by the seeing of Christ. Hebrews calls Jesus' flesh the veil;[160] the flesh (body)[161] of the Adamic man that he took upon Himself in order to die. He took the veil of the flesh of humanity to the Cross and put it away or took it out of the way.

The lack of confidence that is evident in the Church proceeds from an evil conscience. What takes place in the soul that waits unto His coming? The soul is purged from an evil conscience and we, with the full assurance (confidence) of faith come to apprehend the New and

---

[160] Hebrews 10:19-22
Having therefore, brethren, boldness to enter into the holiest by the blood of Jesus, By a new and living way, which he hath consecrated for us, through the veil, that is to say, his flesh; And having an high priest over the house of God; Let us draw near with a true heart in full assurance of faith, having our hearts sprinkled from an evil conscience, and our bodies washed with pure water.

[161] Hebrews 10:5-7
Wherefore when he cometh into the world, he saith, Sacrifice and offering thou wouldest not, but a body hast thou prepared me: In burnt offerings and sacrifices for sin thou hast had no pleasure. Then said I, Lo, I come (in the volume of the book it is written of me,) to do thy will, O God.

Living reality that Christ has procured for us. We behold a perfect salvation, without reference to sin, or better stated, without reference to the veil of humanity. In such a clear cut, we will never be compelled to look in the earth for anything of life and godliness ever again. Our confidence will be fixed solely in Christ due to the conscience now being freed from the remnants of the old and the first that we attempted to carry over into Christ. This judgment brings about clarity and permits the soul finally to observe salvation without sin, without reference to Adam, without reference to flesh and blood; the soul finally beholds salvation without it being shrouded in the veil of self. Christ all and in all is now the view and fixed perspective of the heart and the sole object of a Spirit guided pursuit.

The salvation we have in Christ is fully and sufficiently spiritual. It does not need religious supplementation; it does demand the enlightenment of the soul. First the natural, afterward the Spiritual. When something of the first, something of the earthly remains in our soul's residual memory, we will, without fail create an image and attribute God's name and identity to what is merely familiar to ourselves. In other words, we will attempt to put an earthly identity and form upon what is altogether Spirit and Truth. I was reading in Deuteronomy Chapter 4 and what is said there became a real warning.

Deuteronomy 4:12-20, *"And the Lord spake unto you out of the midst of the fire: ye heard the voice of the words, but saw no similitude; only ye heard a voice. And he declared unto you his covenant, which he commanded you to perform, even ten commandments; and he wrote them upon two tables of stone. And the Lord commanded me at that time to teach you statutes and judgments, that ye might do them in the land whither ye go over to possess it. Take ye therefore good heed unto yourselves; for ye saw no manner of similitude on the day that the Lord spake unto you in Horeb out of the midst of the fire: Lest ye corrupt yourselves, and make you a graven image, the similitude of any figure, the likeness of male or female, The likeness of any beast that is on the earth, the likeness of any winged fowl that flieth in the air, The likeness of any thing that creepeth on the ground, the likeness of any fish that is in the waters beneath the earth: And lest thou lift up thine eyes unto heaven, and when thou seest the sun, and the moon, and the stars, even all the host of heaven, shouldest be driven to worship them, and serve them, which the Lord thy God hath divided unto all nations under the whole heaven. But the Lord hath taken you, and brought you forth out of the iron furnace, even out of Egypt, to be unto him a people of inheritance, as ye are this day."* I recognize this as a real situation in the church world today. God is reminding them that when He made Himself known to them it was not in an outward semblance or similitude. God did not show them a form by which they could know Him. They could not look at God and say He looks like a man or a bull. He did not appear to them in an image, so He is warning them not to put an earthly image before them and call it God. A similitude is a form and it speaks of something that is similar, a simile. We have a facsimile these days. It is not the thing itself but it does look similar. The copy looks like the original. It means similar, a simile, a counterpart, something that is comparable. In other words, God is saying, "I am not comparable to anything you can see with your eyes and the moment you attempt to make me such, you have corrupted yourselves." Notice, they do not corrupt God, but themselves. They make an animal; He is not comparable to that. He is altogether other than that. They make an image of a man or a woman. God has no resemblance to that. Humanity is not the counterpart or the facsimile of God. God has no counterpart. God has nothing in the earth that is in any way similar to who He is.

We are dealing with natural men attempting to make God according to their own image or imagination. God's warning is concerning taking our view and attempting to define God by it. Is that not what we do? We imagine what spiritual reality looks like. What does righteousness look like? Then a man with a natural image comes in and creates an image; righteousness looks like a woman without makeup or a man laying down the cigarettes for Jesus. We have a million different denominations based upon their concept of what it looks like. Some of them base it upon what we wear, where we go, what we do, or what we eat. That is in no way comparable to the righteousness eternally defined of God in the Son who is our righteousness. I promise you, if we see the Lord, we will understand His otherness. We will understand that He is in no way similar to us.

That is why the ark must be seen as afar off from us. We have come to a reality that is not familiar. We have come to a land to which we have never been. We have never known this before. We cannot. It is foreign to us. To attempt to bring something of the natural in and say, "This is what God looks like; here's what righteousness is," is to do nothing more that build and worship an image. God is saying to us, '"LET ME SHOW YOU WHO I AM. Let me reveal myself." In the revealing of Christ, we will see righteousness but we will see it without sin. We will not lose righteousness, but our concept of it that is according to our vain imaginations. We will see a salvation that does not have the face of man as its evidence or measure. That is why to those who look for Him, He appears without sin. He appears, as the salvation that has not the stain of flesh, has not the stain of that which falls short. He desires to reveal a salvation perfectly and eternally defined in the Son of His Love. That is the salvation we must stand still and see. If this is not the ongoing work of God in us, we have the tendency to throw our confidence away because we will long to see the reality of God in ourselves.

The Cross was not a copy machine that produced carbon copies of Christ. The Cross ripped up the piece of paper upon which we were drawing our perverse pictures like little children. The Cross took out the man of flesh and raised up One Man of Spirit and He is Christ all and in all. Only One remains and He has no earthly or natural equivalent. Salvation is not about little facsimiles or being comparable with Jesus; it is the Original Intention and Substance living in the soul and being revealed in the soul. He must be ever before us as the single object of our pursuit.

When you read the things God lists in Deuteronomy 4, in view of which they could make images, does it sound familiar? It should bring you back to the Genesis account of creation. It is all the things that God created, that pertained to a natural creation. You cannot observe the reality of a New Creation or newness of Life within the context of a natural creation. Notice what God says to them. *"And lest thou lift up thine eyes unto heaven, and when thou seest the sun, and the moon, and the stars, even all the host of heaven, shouldest be driven to worship them, and serve them,* **which the Lord thy God hath divided unto all nations under the whole heaven.** *But the Lord hath taken you, and brought you forth out of the iron furnace, even out of Egypt, to be unto him a people of inheritance, as ye are this day."* This is vital. This is the problem with the Church world. These natural things were accessible and observable to **all nations** under the whole heavens. In other words, these things are accessible to everyone on the face of the earth. God had called Israel out unto Himself. Their comprehension of who He is should be much greater than the heathen. Their view of God should not be the same as the world, as mere men. Do you see the parallel? The comprehension of God that most born again people possess is rarely different from the world. God would reveal in our hearts His own vision, so we see a reality that is far removed from a naturally observed creation. Is your view of Life and Righteousness and Salvation different from the other Gentiles? Is your soul beholding the Life and salvation that is revealed by the Father and is hidden from the carnal reasoning of mere men? If our souls are not having the spiritual perfection of the Son of God revealed within, we will still attempt to look in a natural creation to define eternal fullness. Paul warns in Ephesians 4:17-18, *"This I say therefore, and testify in the Lord, that ye henceforth walk not as other Gentiles walk, in the vanity of their mind, Having the understanding darkened, being alienated from the life of God through the ignorance that is in them, because of the blindness of their heart."* This is how most of us are still walking. Vanity of vanities. Everything under the sun is vanity; everything that is not revealed from and eternally defined in heaven is vanity. The mind of man cannot look at anything beyond the vanity that is under the sun. Just as we examined in Peter, the blindness of the heart is the self-aware view of the natural mind, attempting to measure and define the Divine Nature by observing the natural face of men. This causes us to live in a state of alienation from His Life and keeps us bound to our feeble and perverse attempts to imitate His Life with our own. What a bondage to the heart. That is the root and the means of an evil conscience.

I want to end this book by looking at the conscience. Again, Hebrews 10 speaks of having our hearts purged from an evil conscience. The evil conscience is that understanding of salvation that is attached to the first that has been put away. It is still affixed to that which falls short. It is still attached to that which never brought pleasure to the heart of

God. When we have such a conscience, we are trying to relate to God within the context of something that has never pleased Him, that He does not relate to at all. That is an evil conscience. It's a conscience linked to what is evil. What is evil is not the things we do that are deemed as bad, but the wretched man we are out from which we attempt to please God. Evil is anything that still has you and me as the object or measure and definition. An evil conscience is one that perceives the Cross as a means to become like Jesus; such still has us as the object.

The scripture also speaks of a good conscience. So what is a good conscience? 1 Peter 3:18-22, *"For Christ also hath once suffered for sins, the just for the unjust, that he might bring us to God, being put to death in the flesh, but quickened by the Spirit: By which also he went and preached unto the Spirits in prison; Which sometime were disobedient, when once the longsuffering of God waited in the days of Noah, while the ark was a preparing, wherein few, that is, eight souls were saved by water. The like figure whereunto even baptism doth also now save us (not the putting away of the filth of the flesh, but the answer of a good conscience toward God,) by the resurrection of Jesus Christ: Who is gone into heaven, and is on the right hand of God; angels and authorities and powers being made subject unto him."*

The like figure whereunto even baptism doth also now save us. This baptism is the means of possessing the answer of a good conscience toward God. We must understand that Peter is not referring to water baptism. Noah was not a type and a figure of water baptism. He was a type and figure of the greater baptism, which is being baptized into the death of Christ. This baptism doth now save us. Peter then says this little phrase that encompasses the resulting realization of this baptism we encounter. This is very important to understand about this baptism; it is *"not the putting away of the filth of the flesh, but the answer of a good conscience toward God by the resurrection of Jesus Christ."* Here is what our baptism has done and if we will allow that baptism, the death of Christ, that true baptism, to work in our hearts here is the inward result. It again is about God's view being wrought within and the effect of it. I repeat, the confidence of your heart is always linked to the condition of the conscience. Where your conscience is your confidence is. If your conscience is linked to flesh and blood, your confidence is linked to flesh and blood. If your conscience is linked to Christ, your confidence is linked to Christ.

That is a simple way of saying it; I will try to explain. Peter speaks of Noah, and when we look at Noah, we are seeing the taking away of one creation and the establishing of a New Creation in One Man. Here is the inward working of that. The inward working of that doth now save us. That is our salvation. However, this baptism is not just the washing of your flesh. It has nothing to do with just getting rid of the dirt and filth of your flesh or getting rid of outward things. It is not that, it is not outward. It is about your conscience being purged. This is the conscience being purged with pure water, the waters of the true baptism where one is put away and One remains. It is about your conscience being brought into line with the reality embodied and established in Christ. According to Peter, this good conscience is according to the resurrection. What is that? Christ liveth in me. Not I, but Christ liveth in me as my Life. It is about the Life of the soul appearing and all that is not life being reckoned to be the death that it is.[162] It

---

[162] Romans 6:3-11
Know ye not, that so many of us as were baptized into Jesus Christ were baptized into his death? Therefore we are buried with him by baptism into death: that like as Christ was raised up from the dead by the glory of the

is Christ declaring in your soul: "I Am the One who lives. I Am the Resurrection. I Am the Life. I Am the Living One." That is the resurrection. That is my soul knowing the resurrection. This answer of a good conscience is directly related and inseparably bound to the inward knowing and experiencing of the One who is The Resurrection.

We must now look at the word conscience for a moment, because the familiar usage of this word can cause you to misunderstand what I am attempting to say. Conscience in the Greek is made up of two words: σύν sun and εἴδω eido. [163] Sun means united, joined, in union with. [164] Eido means to see, to comprehend, and to understand by seeing.[165]

Father, even so we also should walk in newness of life. For if we have been planted together in the likeness of his death, we shall be also in the likeness of his resurrection: Knowing this, that our old man is crucified with him, that the body of sin might be destroyed, that henceforth we should not serve sin. For he that is dead is freed from sin. Now if we be dead with Christ, we believe that we shall also live with him: Knowing that Christ being raised from the dead dieth no more; death hath no more dominion over him. For in that he died, he died unto sin once: but in that he liveth, he liveth unto God. Likewise reckon ye also yourselves to be dead indeed unto sin, but alive unto God through Jesus Christ our Lord.

[163] NT:4893 συνείδησις suneidesis (soon-i'-day-sis); from a prolonged form of NT:4894; co-perception, i.e. moral consciousness: KJV - conscience. *(Biblesoft's New Exhaustive Strong's Numbers and Concordance with Expanded Greek-Hebrew Dictionary. Copyright © 1994, 2003, 2006 Biblesoft, Inc. and International Bible Translators, Inc.)*

[164] NT:4862 σύν sun (soon); a primary preposition denoting union; with or together. *(Biblesoft's New Exhaustive Strong's Numbers and Concordance with Expanded Greek-Hebrew Dictionary. Copyright © 1994, 2003, 2006 Biblesoft, Inc. and International Bible Translators, Inc.)*

[165] NT:1492 εἴδω eido (i'-do); a primary verb; used only in certain past tenses, the others being borrowed from the equivalent NT:3700 and NT:3708; properly, to see (literally or figuratively); by implication (in the perf. only) to know: KJV - be aware, behold, can (+not tell), consider, (have) know (-ledge), look (on), perceive, see, be sure, tell, understand, wish, wot. *(Biblesoft's New Exhaustive Strong's Numbers and Concordance with*

Therefore, when we read of the conscience, we are speaking of an understanding that is joined or united with something or someone. It is an understanding that is joined to that which we are beholding. In other words, the state of the conscience is directly related to the reality or illusion upon which the sight of our soul is fixed. So, what does this have to do with the resurrection or Noah?

We now go to the Genesis account of the flood to see this. Genesis 6:5-18, *"And God saw that the wickedness of man was great in the earth, and that every imagination of the thoughts of his heart was only evil continually. And it repented the Lord that he had made man on the earth, and it grieved him at his heart. And the Lord said, I will destroy man whom I have created from the face of the earth; both man, and beast, and the creeping thing, and the fowls of the air; for it repenteth me that I have made them. But Noah found grace in the eyes of the Lord. These are the generations of Noah: Noah was a just man and perfect in his generations, and Noah walked with God. And Noah begat three sons, Shem, Ham, and Japheth. The earth also was corrupt before God, and the earth was filled with violence. And God looked upon the earth, and, behold, it was corrupt; for all flesh had corrupted his way upon the earth. And God said unto Noah, The end of all flesh is come before me; for the earth is filled with violence through them; and, behold, I will destroy them with the earth. Make thee an ark of gopher wood; rooms shalt thou make in the ark, and shalt pitch it within and without with pitch. And this is the fashion which thou shalt make it of: The length of the ark shall be three hundred cubits, the breadth of it fifty cubits, and the height of it thirty cubits. A window shalt thou make to the ark, and in a cubit shalt thou finish it*

Expanded Greek-Hebrew Dictionary. Copyright © 1994, 2003, 2006 Biblesoft, Inc. and International Bible Translators, Inc.)

above; and the door of the ark shalt thou set in the side thereof; with lower, second, and third stories shalt thou make it. And, behold, I, even I, do bring a flood of waters upon the earth, to destroy all flesh, wherein is the breath of life, from under heaven; and every thing that is in the earth shall die. But with thee will I establish my covenant; and thou shalt come into the ark, thou, and thy sons, and thy wife, and thy sons' wives with thee." Genesis 7:1, *"And the Lord said unto Noah, Come thou and all thy house into the ark; for thee have I seen righteous before me in this generation."* God sees man and sees that his heart and its intents are evil continually. That means there is never a moment when that is not the case with reference to mankind. So, that man grieves the heart of God, God's pleasure is not found in that man at all. But there is ONE MAN who finds grace in His sight. One stands before God as righteous and upright. It is that man with whom God makes this New Covenant and in whom a New Creation will be named and identified. By this flood, this baptism, one creation, and humanity are totally put away and destroyed. After that destruction was accomplished, the scripture is very clear in stating the reality of the New Creation and the view of God. Genesis 7:21-23, *"And all flesh died that moved upon the earth, both of fowl, and of cattle, and of beast, and of every creeping thing that creepeth upon the earth, and every man: All in whose nostrils was the breath of life, of all that was in the dry land, died. And every living substance was destroyed which was upon the face of the ground, both man, and cattle, and the creeping things, and the fowl of the heaven; and they were destroyed from the earth: and* **Noah only remained alive***, and they that were with him in the ark."* Peter says eight were saved, but this truly defines that there was One who remained and those who were in union with him. Because He lived, they lived also. He remained and they remained by being of his household. The New Creation is not measured by dead men or living men. The New Creation is ONE MAN living as the Life of all who will live. This is the Resurrection.

In newness of Life, nothing of the first remains. The One righteous in God's eyes; the One who is the sight and view of God remains and He is the Head of a New Creation. The Covenant is sure in the One who remains. When we attempt to define something of our Life in Christ, in view of that which has been removed by the Cross, we have missed the reality. We still have a heart that has been corrupted from the simplicity that God beholds in the face of One. This is what it means to have the answer of a good conscience by the resurrection. Peter is speaking of a conscience that is no longer affixed to what God has put away. This is the circumcision of the heart addressed in the last chapter. The soul's comprehension of salvation is no longer affixed to the man or creation that the flood has washed away. The soul's view and understanding is inseparably joined to the One who remains; the One who lives in us as the surety of all spiritual fullness. Peter is writing of a conscience that is fixed, that is set within that which is New and spiritual, within the boundaries of union with the One with whom God has made His eternal covenant. A good conscience beholds the New that has come and is experiencing inwardly the passing away and purging of the old things that are passed away. It is in this understanding that we know no man or even Christ in accordance with flesh. If this baptism is not inwardly effectual, we will attempt to continue to know in that way, when God only sees One who is Spirit and Truth. There is the necessity of a new knowing, a new seeing, and a new comprehension in this New Creation. God reveals the reality of the New by His Spirit; it is never observed by what we perceive with our natural eye.

A good conscience is that which is united to an eternally fixed and certain reality in which there are no variables or shadows of turning.[166] No matter what is around, no matter the ignorance that may prevail in the midst; our soul is anchored in the fullness of spiritual substance. The heart is either fixed upon the variableness of men, their activities, things that may or may not happen, manifestations that may occur one day and not occur the next, or it is joined to and beholding the eternally fixed and sure perfection of the Son who remains the satisfaction of the Father within. How does this conscience actually become the reality in which we live? GOD REVEALS THE SON IN US.

This revealing of Christ brings about the inward working of this awesome baptism and leaves us with much more than cleaned up flesh. The revealing of Christ brings the soul face to face with a salvation without reference to flesh or sin and it leaves a comprehension that is united to Spirit and Truth. The answer of a good conscience in the midst of all things and situations is, NOT I BUT CHRIST LIVES IN ME. The word "answer" is actually an interrogation. That means that in whatever situation, in the mist of whatever accusation or interrogation, whether by man or the enemy, we have the answer that proceeds from a conscience that is joined to the proper Man. To any accusation, our answer is the same: *"One lives here, it is very good, the Father's view is certain and I am not the object or measure of His view."* When that is the state of the conscience, the confidence is there to wait with patience unto His coming. We realize that if there is something of reality that seems to be missing, we will not look outside of His countenance for it. We wait on His appearing as the reality that seemed to be lacking.

---

[166] James 1:17
Every good gift and every perfect gift is from above, and cometh down from the Father of lights, with whom is no variableness, neither shadow of turning.

This is the inward effect of the revealing of the Father's view. In that view, we reckon dead and suffer the loss of what is already put away and invalid, and we grow in the knowledge of the grace of God by which we have been united to the Divine Life and Substance who stands before the Father as His Eternal Pleasure. May this be the continual realization of our hearts, that instead of peering into the face of the Adamic man or the earthly pursuits of religion to find anything, our souls will be forever settled, fixed and established, by faith, within the confines of our union with the revealed Son of God's own satisfaction.

Made in the USA
Charleston, SC
17 February 2014